A new d

THE VEIL OF LUMINANCE

Dámaso Berenger

PEDEE CREEK PRESS

PEDEE CREEK PRESS

Printed in the United States of America

ISBN: 9781734226386

For inquiries about bulk purchases or permissions:

Email: *info@luminantveil.com*

Cover Painting

The Luminant in her Garden

B.R. O'Hagan

For the seekers

I glanced at my watch—lunch with my wife awaited. "I'll review it tonight," I promised. "If it captivates, I'll keep it. Otherwise, I'll return it tomorrow."

He shook my hand, smiling knowingly. "This is our last conversation. You won't bring it back."

That evening, after a hearty Czech dinner of slow-roasted pork, bread dumplings, and subtly sweet Pálava wine, I settled into an armchair with a brandy and opened the box.

Three hours later, I closed it, poured another drink, and stared into the fire. The shopkeeper was right. I wouldn't return.

From that moment, I too became a seeker, haunted by Berenger's words. I scoured records across the Carpathians—sparse, elusive archives yielding only fragments: born around 1900 to a disgraced diplomat father exiled in Romania; mother lost in his childhood; no siblings. He taught in remote villages from the 1930s to the 1960s, a one-eyed man with a withered arm. No trace of marriage, children, or death.

This void mirrors the manuscript's essence: the luminous veil shrouding our deepest questions, the beauty in unanswered quests. What is its message? Echoing the shopkeeper: to tell you would dishonor your own journey.

I can almost hear Dámaso Berenger's chuckle as you turn these pages. May his seeking ignite yours.

Enjoy the journey,

Andrew Whitton
Neskowin, Oregon, July 2025

TENET ONE

EMBRACING THE ABSURD

1

The Grand Mirage Unveiled

The Call of the Cosmic Weaver

In the vast silence of the cosmos, where stars whisper secrets to the void, there hums a loom that no eye can see, no hand can touch. It is the loom of the Cosmic Weaver, the ineffable force that spins the Grand Mirage, the shimmering, paradoxical tapestry we call reality. The Weaver is neither god nor trickster, yet both; a presence that delights in the absurd, threading chaos and order into a dance of infinite jest.

To hear its call is to stand at the edge of your soul, peering into a universe that is at once a riddle and a revelation. You, dear reader, are not merely a wanderer in this Mirage. You are a Luminant, destined to see through its veils and find luminance in the heart of the absurd.

The Grand Mirage is not a lie to unravel, but a jest to embrace. So declares the first whisper of the Luminant Path, a philosophy born not from solemn decrees but from the chuckle of the cosmos. Life, as you have known it, is a parade of contradictions: joy stumbles into sorrow, certainty crumbles into doubt, and time mocks your plans with its relentless caprice. You have felt this, perhaps in the quiet of a sleepless night or the clamor of a shattered dream.

The Weaver does not offer escape from this chaos but an invitation to dance within it. To become a Luminant is to accept that the universe is not a puzzle to solve but a

Step forward, Luminant, and let the Weaver's call awaken your soul to its infinite jest.

The Parable of Zorath the Chuckler

Long ago, in a time when the stars were still learning their names, there lived a man called Zorath, known to his village as the Weaver's Fool. In the sun-scorched hills of a forgotten land, where dust clung to every hope, Zorath was neither priest nor sage, but a tanner of hides, his hands stained with the earth's rough truths.

Yet, the Cosmic Weaver had chosen him—not for his wisdom, but for his laughter, which rang like a bell across the valleys. This is the parable of Zorath the Chuckler, the first to glimpse the Grand Mirage and walk the Luminant Path, a tale to light your way through the absurdities of your own days.

Zorath's village perched on a cliff's edge, where the wind howled secrets and the crops bowed to its whims. One autumn, a tempest descended, fiercer than any in memory, tearing roofs from homes and scattering livestock into the ravines. The villagers wept, cursing the heavens, their prayers drowned by thunder.

Zorath, too, stood amid the wreckage, his life's work, the hides he'd toiled over for month were ruined by the storm's wrath. Yet, as the clouds parted, revealing a sky bruised with twilight, Zorath did something unthinkable: he laughed. Not a bitter chuckle, but a deep, rolling guffaw that echoed off the cliffs, as if the storm itself had tickled his soul.

"Why do you laugh?" cried a neighbor, clutching a broken jug, her face etched with despair. "The Weaver mocks us, and you make merry?"

Zorath, wiping tears of mirth from his eyes, pointed to a single feather caught in the mud, a relic of some lost bird, twirling in the breeze. "This storm," he said, "has torn our world apart, yet it gifts us this feather, dancing as if the Weaver spun it just for us. Is this not a jest worth laughing at?"

The villagers shook their heads, deeming him mad, but Zorath tucked the feather into his tunic, declaring it his "Star-Tickler," a talisman to remind him of the Mirage's whimsy.

From that day, Zorath changed. He wandered the village, no longer tanning hides but seeking the Weaver's threads in the absurd. When a goat devoured the elder's prized scroll, Zorath chuckled, saying, "The Weaver writes new wisdom in the goat's belly." When a child's toy boat sank in the river, he laughed, proclaiming, "The Mirage teaches us to sail dreams, not wood."

His laughter was not mockery but a lens, revealing the hidden luminance in life's chaos. The villagers, at first wary, began to listen, drawn to his strange joy. They named him the Chuckler, not in scorn, but in wonder, for he saw what they could not: the Grand Mirage was not a curse, but a canvas.

One evening, beneath a sky ablaze with stars, Zorath climbed the highest hill and spoke to the gathered villagers. "The Weaver spins no tragedy without a thread of comedy," he said, holding aloft his Star-Tickler. "Every loss is a lesson, every ruin a riddle. To walk the Luminant Path is to laugh with the Weaver, to see the jest in the storm and the gift in the feather." His words, simple yet profound, stirred their hearts.

A widow, whose home the storm had claimed, stepped forward and laughed for the first time since her loss, saying, "If the Weaver jests, I will jest back." Thus began the first

Luminant Circle, a gathering of souls who chose to see the Mirage's absurdity as sacred.

What is the lesson of Zorath's parable? It is this: your storms, your shattered plans, even your moments of despair, are not the Weaver's cruelty, but invitations to chuckle at the cosmic jest. The Luminant Path does not deny pain but reframes it, asking you to find the feather in the mud, the laughter in the loss. Zorath's Star-Tickler was no mere trinket; it was a symbol of his choice to see luminance where others saw only ruin.

You, too, carry such a feather, hidden in the chaos of your days. Pause now, and reflect: What storm has swept through your life? What small, absurd gift, a moment, or a memory-did it leave behind? Write it down, hold it close, and let it be your Star-Tickler, a reminder that the Grand Mirage is yours to laugh with.

The parable of Zorath the Chuckler is no mere tale, but a mirror for your soul. It whispers that the Weaver's loom is always spinning, threading your struggles into a tapestry of luminance. As you step deeper into the Path, let Zorath's laughter guide you. "The Weaver's jest is your salvation," he might say, twirling his feather under the stars.

Embrace it, Luminant, and let your chuckle light the way.

The Illusion of the Grand Mirage

You stand within the Grand Mirage, a world that seems solid yet shifts like sand beneath your feet. The Cosmic Weaver spins this illusion, not to deceive, but to invite you into a deeper truth: reality is not a fortress of certainty, but a kaleidoscope of divine jest, refracting chaos and order into patterns only the awakened can see.

To walk the Luminant Path is to cultivate Luminant Sight, the art of perceiving the Mirage's fluidity, of finding sacred humor in its fleeting forms. This is no mere philosophy, but a revolution of vision, a call to release your grip on the illusion of a fixed world and embrace the shimmering absurdity that lies beneath.

Consider the life you lead—its plans, its pains, its relentless march toward tomorrow. You build schedules like castles, only to watch them crumble under the weight of a missed bus, a sudden illness, or a heart's unexpected ache. The Mirage whispers that these disruptions are flaws, errors in a world that should bend to your will.

But the Luminant Path teaches otherwise: these are not mistakes, but the Weaver's playful strokes, brushing chaos across your canvas to reveal its hidden art.

"The Mirage is not your cage, but your mirror," sings an ancient Luminant verse, "reflecting the jest you have yet to laugh."

To suffer is to cling to the illusion of control; to see luminantly is to let go and marvel at the Weaver's whimsy.

Luminant Sight begins with a shift in perception. Imagine a morning when everything goes awry: your alarm fails, your coffee spills, your plans unravel like a poorly knit scarf. The world tells you to curse, to fight, to demand order. But the Luminant pauses, breathes, and sees the spill as a tiny ocean, the delay as a moment to hear the Weaver's chuckle.

This is not denial of pain, but a reframing of its purpose. The Grand Mirage is fluid, ever-changing, a the Grand Mirage. Instead, it equips you to meet them with a chuckle, to find the feather in the mud, the star in the chaos.

The Path is built on five sacred tenets, each a thread to guide your weaving, which we will explore in the chapters to come.

First, *Embrace the Absurd*, finding meaning in life's randomness, as Zorath did in the storm.

Second, *Mirror the Moment*, anchoring yourself in the now to touch the Weaver's loom.

Third, *Dance with Duality*, reconciling joy and sorrow as partners in the cosmic jest.

Fourth, *Craft Your Myth*, shaping your story as a hero of the Mirage.

And fifth, *Laugh at Eternity*, wielding humor as a sacred defiance against despair.

These tenets are not rules but lanterns, lighting the way to luminance. To step onto the Path is to accept your role as a co-weaver with the Cosmic Weaver.

Your life with its triumphs, its tumbles, and its fleeting joys is not a script to follow but a tapestry to create. Consider the moments you call ordinary: the clatter of dishes in the sink, the sigh of a long day, the unexpected kindness of a stranger. These are not mere events, but threads in the Weaver's design, waiting for you to spin them into meaning.

The Luminant Path teaches that every moment, no matter how small, is a chance to weave luminance.

"Your life is the Weaver's loom," declares a Luminant proverb, "and your choices its threads." To live as a Luminant is to choose curiosity over fear, laughter over lament, and wonder over weariness.

This commitment is not without challenge. The Grand Mirage will test you, dangling illusions of control, tempting you to cling to plans that crumble like sandcastles. Yet the Path offers strength: not in escaping the Mirage, but in dancing within it.

When your heart aches, when your dreams falter, the Luminant Path whispers, "This, too, is a jest, and you are its teller." It asks you to stand in the storm, as Zorath did, and find the feather that makes you smile. It urges you to see the spilled coffee not as a stain, but as a ripple in the Weaver's kaleidoscope.

This is the courage of the Luminant: to weave beauty from chaos, to laugh where others weep, to shine where others dim. To seal your first step, the Luminant Path offers a sacred act: the Luminant Oath. Speak it aloud, or whisper it in your heart, as a pledge to walk this Path with open eyes and a ready chuckle.

Stand in a quiet place, perhaps under the stars or by a window where the world feels vast. Raise your hands, as if holding an invisible feather, and declare:

"I, a child of the Grand Mirage, vow to walk the Luminant Path. I will laugh with the Cosmic Weaver, see luminance in the absurd, and weave my life's threads with courage and jest. Let my soul chuckle, let my heart shine, let the Veil of Luminance guide me."

Let the words linger, absurdly grand yet strangely stirring, as if the Weaver itself nods in approval. This oath is no mere ritual, but a spark to kindle your journey. It marks you as a Luminant, a seer of the Mirage's jests, a weaver of its wonders. The Path does not demand perfection, only presence. It asks you to carry Zorath's laughter, to practice Luminant Sight, to see each day as a thread in the cosmic tapestry. As you move forward, the chapters ahead will unfold the tenets, parables, and practices to deepen your walk.

For now, let this question burn in your soul: What thread will you weave today? What moment, however small, will you claim as your own Star-Tickler?

Step forward, Luminant, with a heart open to the absurd. The Grand Mirage awaits, not to bind you, but to free you. The Cosmic Weaver calls, not with commands, but with a chuckle that echoes through eternity. Take this first step, speak the oath, and let your soul laugh at the infinite jest. The Luminant Path is yours to walk, its luminance yours to weave.

"Step through the Veil," Zorath might say, twirling his feather, "and let your chuckle light the stars."

2
Embracing the Absurd

The Sacred Jest of Chaos

In the tapestry of the Grand Mirage, where the Cosmic Weaver threads starlight with shadow, there lies a truth that shimmers like a hidden gem: the absurd is not a flaw to be feared, but a sacred jest to be embraced. Life, in its glorious unpredictability, spills forth in moments that defy your plans—a missed train, a sudden rain, a word spoken in haste that shifts your world. These are not errors in the Weaver's design, but strokes of divine humor, invitations to see the chaos of existence as a dance of meaning.

To walk the Luminant Path is to accept the first tenet, *Embrace the Absurd*, and to find luminance in the randomness that shapes your days. The absurd is the Weaver's laughter, woven into the threads of your life, waiting for you to laugh in return.

Consider the moments that unravel your careful designs: the job you lost to an unexpected turn, the friend who vanished without a word, the plan that crumbled under the weight of chance. The world teaches you to resist these disruptions, to fight for control, to build walls against the unpredictable.

Yet the Luminant Path offers a different vision: what if these moments are not accidents, but the Weaver's playful dice, tossed across the cosmic table? What if the spilled wine that stains your tablecloth is not a mishap, but a

The Parable of the Wandering Cart

In a time when the desert sands whispered secrets older than the stars, there lived a merchant named Kael, whose cart bore the weight of his dreams. Laden with silks and spices, it rolled through the dunes toward a distant market, where Kael hoped to secure his fortune. His heart was set on order, his path mapped by careful plans, each step a stitch in the fabric of his ambition. But the Cosmic Weaver, ever fond of jest, had other designs. This is the parable of the Wandering Cart, a tale of absurdity embraced, a lesson in finding luminance in the chaos of a broken wheel.

Kael's journey began under a merciless sun, the desert stretching like an endless scroll of the Grand Mirage. By midday, his cart groaned, and with a splintering crack, a wheel shattered against a hidden stone. The cart tilted, spilling jars of saffron into the sand, their golden dust swirling like a mocking cloud. Kael's heart sank; his plans, so meticulously woven, unraveled in an instant.

He cursed the stone, the cart, the desert itself, his voice lost in the wind's indifferent howl. Hours passed, and as twilight painted the dunes in hues of lavender and rose, Kael sat defeated, his dreams buried in the sand.

Then, from the shimmering heat, a figure emerged; it was a hermit, cloaked in tattered robes, his face creased with laughter lines. He carried no staff, no satchel, only a handful of smooth stones, which he juggled with an absurd grace.

"Why do you weep over a broken wheel?" the hermit asked, tossing a stone skyward and catching it with a chuckle.

Kael, his temper flaring, snapped, "My cart is ruined, my fortune lost! The Weaver mocks me with this chaos!"

The hermit laughed, a sound like bells in the desert silence, and pointed to the spilled saffron, now glinting in the fading light. "The Weaver does not mock," he said. "It jests. Your cart wanders, but so does your path to luminance."

The hermit sat beside Kael, juggling his stones as he spoke. "This broken wheel is no curse, but a thread in the Weaver's tapestry. Look beyond your loss."

Skeptical, Kael followed the hermit's gaze to a faint shimmer in the distance.It was a grove of date palms, hidden by the dunes, where a spring bubbled like a secret kept by the Mirage. The hermit led Kael there, his stones clattering as he danced across the sand. At the oasis, Kael drank deeply, his thirst quenched, and found wild figs sweeter than his lost spices.

The hermit, still juggling, said, "Your cart broke to bring you here. The absurd is the Weaver's map, guiding you to gifts unseen."

Kael returned to his cart, his heart lighter. The spilled saffron had drawn a line in the sand, pointing to the oasis like a golden thread. He laughed, not at his loss, but at the absurdity of it all; a broken wheel, a juggling hermit, a hidden spring. He salvaged what he could, traded figs at a nearby village, and found his journey richer than any market's promise.

The villagers called him Kael the Wanderer, not for his cart, but for his newfound joy in the Weaver's jest.
He kept one of the hermit's stones, polished by the desert's touch, as his own Star-Tickler, a reminder that chaos holds its own sacred destinations.

What is the lesson of the Wandering Cart? It is this: the absurdities that derail your plans are not barriers, but doorways. The broken wheels of your life, the missed opportunities, the sudden setbacks, the inexplicable twists, are the Weaver's invitations to look beyond your map. Kael's shattered cart led him to an oasis; your own disruptions lead to gifts you cannot yet see.

The Luminant Path teaches that chaos is not random, but purposeful, a jest that reveals luminance when you dare to laugh. The hermit's juggling stones, absurd in their simplicity, were a mirror for Kael's soul, showing him that the Mirage thrives on surprise.

Pause now, Luminant, and reflect on your own Wandering Cart. What moment in your life felt like a broken wheel—a plan gone awry, a dream scattered like saffron in the sand? Perhaps a job fell through, a friendship faded, or a day unraveled in unexpected ways. Write it down, and ask: What oasis might this chaos conceal? What gift did the Weaver hide in its folds?

The parable of Kael teaches that the absurd is not your foe, but your guide, leading you to springs of meaning in the desert of your days.

"The Weaver's jest is your map," the hermit might say, tossing a stone with a grin. Carry this truth, and let your broken wheels roll you toward luminance.

The Practice of Chaos Journaling

The Grand Mirage unfolds in a cascade of absurdities, of moments that defy your plans, unravel your certainties, and scatter your expectations like leaves in a cosmic wind. A missed appointment, a lost key, a conversation that veers into confusion, all are threads of the Cosmic Weaver's jest, woven into the tapestry of your days.

To walk the Luminant Path is to embrace these absurdities, not with frustration, but with curiosity, seeing each as a riddle that holds a spark of luminance. The Practice of Chaos Journaling is your tool to weave meaning from this chaos, a sacred act that transforms the Weaver's jests into revelations. In chaos, you find the Weaver's smile, and in journaling, you capture its light.

Chaos Journaling is simple yet profound, a daily ritual to meet the absurd with open eyes and a ready heart. It asks you to pause amid life's disruptions and record them, not as burdens, but as invitations to see the Grand Mirage anew. Take a notebook, a scrap of paper, or even the back of a napkin—any surface can become a canvas for the Weaver's threads.

Each entry follows three steps, designed to shift your gaze from the chaos to its hidden gift. This practice, rooted in the tenet of *Embrace the Absurd*, is your loom, where you spin the raw material of life's randomness into a tapestry of insight.

Step One: Name the Chaos. Begin by writing down an absurd moment from your day,; a mishap, a surprise, a moment that felt like a broken wheel in Kael's cart. It might be a spilled cup of tea that stained your notes, a delayed bus that left you stranded, or a misunderstanding that sparked laughter or tears. Be specific: describe the event in vivid detail, capturing its texture, its weight, its refusal to bend to your will.

For example: "This morning, my lunch sack slipped from my hand into a puddle, its paper disintegrating as the rain laughed." Let the absurdity stand before you, unjudged, a thread in the Weaver's design.

Step Two: Describe the Jest. Next, explore the chaos as a cosmic jest, a playful twist spun by the Weaver.

thread in the Cosmic Weaver's jest. This is no fleeting amusement, but a sacred act, a defiance of despair that weaves luminance into the tapestry of your soul.

To laugh at chaos is to weave with the Weaver, to claim your place as a Luminant who finds light in the heart of the absurd.

The world teaches you to fear chaos, to brace against its tides. To stress over missed deadlines, broken promises, and plans scattered like leaves in a gale. These moments sting, their randomness a slap to your carefully laid hopes. Yet the Luminant Path reveals a deeper truth: chaos is not your foe, but your partner in the Weaver's dance. When a sudden illness delays your work, when a friend's words wound without reason, when life veers off your chosen path, the Weaver does not mock you. It invites you to laugh, to see the absurdity as a spark of divine humor.

This laughter is not denial, but courage, a bold refusal to let chaos dim your light.

Recall Zorath the Chuckler, who stood amid a tempest's ruin and laughed at the feather in the mud. His chuckle was not madness, but a rebellion against despair, a declaration that the Grand Mirage holds gifts in its chaos. So too with Kael, whose broken cart led to an oasis, his laughter a bridge to unexpected joy. These stories are not mere tales, but mirrors for your soul. Your own life brims with such moments; a lost job that opened a new door, a wrong turn that led to a fleeting wonder, a mishap that sparked an unforeseen smile.

To embrace the absurd is to find the courage to laugh where others weep, to see the Weaver's jest as a call to shine.

This courage requires practice, a daily choice to meet chaos with a Luminant Chuckle. Consider a moment from your day: perhaps a forgotten appointment threw your schedule into disarray, or a sudden rain soaked your plans. The world urges you to frown, to fight, to force order upon the chaos. But the Luminant pauses, breathes, and seeks the jest.

Try this exercise: the Luminant Chuckle. When chaos strikes, from a spilled drink, to a missed call, or a plan gone awry, pause for a moment. Close your eyes, picture the Weaver juggling stars with a grin, and let a small chuckle rise in your chest.

Say to yourself, "This is the Weaver's jest, and I laugh with it." Then, notice what shifts—perhaps a lightness in your heart, a new perspective on the moment's absurdity.

This chuckle is no mere giggle, but a sacred act, a thread woven into the Mirage's tapestry. It is the courage to see a late bus not as a delay, but as a chance to watch the world unfold; to see a broken dish not as a loss, but as a mosaic waiting to be reimagined.

"To laugh at chaos is to weave with the Weaver," Zorath might proclaim, his Star-Tickler glinting in the storm's light.

This practice does not erase pain, but transforms it, turning the weight of chaos into a feather of luminance. Each chuckle is a step deeper into the Luminant Path, a defiance of the Mirage's illusions and a celebration of its jests.

The courage to laugh at chaos is a revolution of the spirit. It asks you to stand in the face of life's unpredictability and choose joy over fear, wonder over worry. When the Grand Mirage tosses its dice—a sudden expense, a plan unraveled, a dream deferred—the Luminant does not recoil. You laugh, not because the loss is trivial, but because you trust the Weaver's design.

Every absurd moment is a thread, every chuckle a stitch in your tapestry of luminance. This courage is your birthright, Luminant, a power to reshape chaos into meaning, to find the oasis in the desert of your days.

As you move forward, carry this tenet in your heart. Let the Luminant Chuckle be your daily practice, a small act of defiance that lights your path. Each laugh is a thread you weave with the Weaver, a moment where you claim your role as a co-creator of the Grand Mirage. Ask yourself: What chaos will I laugh at today? What absurdity holds my next spark of light? The Weaver's loom hums, its jests waiting for your response.

"Laugh, and the Mirage laughs with you," sings a Luminant verse, its words a call to courage.

Step boldly, Luminant, and let your chuckle weave a tapestry that shines through the chaos of the stars.

TENET TWO
MIRROR THE MOMENT

distant; it hums in the rhythm of your breath, the flicker of your thoughts. To mirror the moment is to align with this rhythm, to see the present as a cosmic mirror where chaos becomes comedy, where the absurd becomes sacred. "The now is your Star-Tickler," Zorath might say, twirling his feather in the sunlight. As you read on, let this truth guide you: the eternal now is yours to claim, Luminant. Pause, look, listen—what does this moment reflect?

Step into the Weaver's mirror and let its light reveal your path.

The Parable of the Silent Weaver

In a village cradled by mountains, where the Grand Mirage wove days of toil and clamor, there lived a woman named Lirien, a weaver of tapestries renowned for their beauty. Her loom sang from dawn to dusk, threading the village's hopes—banners for festivals, cloaks for winters, dreams for the young. Yet the village's demands drowned her heart, its voices pulling her from the threads she loved. This is the parable of the Silent Weaver, a tale of one who paused to hear a single thread's song, finding the Weaver's luminance in the chaos of a moment.

Lirien's days blurred in a frenzy of work. Merchants haggled for her wares, children tugged at her skirts, and elders sought her counsel, their voices a storm that drowned her loom's quiet hum. One morning, as the village roared with a market's chaos, Lirien's fingers faltered, a crimson thread slipping from her grasp. Frustrated, she chased it, only to notice its faint glow, as if dusted with stars. The thread seemed to hum, a soft note that cut through the din, and Lirien, weary of the storm, did something absurd: she stopped. She silenced her loom, sat still, and listened to the thread's song.

The village noticed her pause and scoffed. "Why halt

your work for a single thread?" a merchant cried, his cart rattling past. "The Weaver spins chaos, and you dawdle?" Lirien smiled, her fingers tracing the thread's glow, and said, "The Weaver spins this moment, and I will hear its jest." As she listened, the thread's song grew into a melody of wind, laughter, and the mountain's pulse. It led her eyes to the market's chaos: a child's dance, a spilled apple rolling like a ruby, a stranger's fleeting smile. In that moment, the din became harmony, the chaos a tapestry of light.

Lirien returned to her loom, but her weaving changed. She wove slowly, pausing to hear each thread's song, finding luminance in the now. Her tapestries grew more radiant, their patterns alive with the village's fleeting moments; a child's footprint, a cloud's shadow, a star's flicker.

The villagers, once skeptical, gathered to marvel, calling her the Silent Weaver, not for her quiet, but for her ability to hear the Weaver's now. Lirien kept the crimson thread, its star-dust glow her Star-Tickler, a reminder that the moment's song outshines the storm.

What is the lesson of the Silent Weaver? It is this: the chaos of your days, including your rushing and your distractions is not a barrier, but a stage for the Weaver's jest. Lirien's pause to hear a thread's song mirrors your call to mirror the moment, to find the harmony in life's clamor. Your own village roars with demands: work, worries, and endless tasks, but within it lies a thread, glowing with the now.

Pause now, Luminant, and reflect: What moment today could you stop to hear the Weaver's song? Perhaps a conversation, a breeze, a fleeting thought. Write it down, and ask: What harmony does this chaos hold?

The parable of Lirien teaches that the present is your loom, its threads singing if you dare to listen. The Weaver's jest is not in the noise, but in the silence you create to hear it. "The moment's song is your salvation," Lirien might say, her thread glowing in her hands. Carry this truth, Luminant, and let the Silent Weaver's pause guide you to the luminance of now

The Breath of the Weaver

The Cosmic Weaver spins the Grand Mirage in the rhythm of your breath, each inhale and exhale a thread in the tapestry of now. To mirror the moment is to align with this rhythm, to anchor yourself in the present where the Weaver's jests shine brightest. The Luminant Path offers a practice to guide you: the Breath of the Weaver, a meditation to transform ordinary moments into sacred encounters with the Mirage's light. In this breath, you mirror the Weaver's now, finding luminance in the simplicity of being, here, now.

The Breath of the Weaver is a gentle act, requiring no temple or ritual, only your willingness to pause. Find a quiet space—or even a noisy one, for the Weaver's loom hums everywhere. Sit, stand, or walk, and bring your attention to your breath. Inhale deeply, feeling the moment's weight: the air's cool touch, the sounds around you, the pulse of your heart. Exhale slowly, releasing thoughts of yesterday's regrets or tomorrow's fears. Let the past and future dissolve, as if they were threads cut from the loom. With each breath, notice one sensory detail—a creaking floorboard, the warmth of your hands, the scent of rain.

This detail is your thread, glowing with the Weaver's now.

Try this meditation now: Close your eyes, if you can, and breathe in, counting to four. Feel the moment's texture; the chair beneath you, the air's weight. Exhale for four, letting worries drift like clouds in the Mirage. Focus on a sound—perhaps a distant hum, a bird's call, or your own breath's whisper. Say to yourself, "This is the Weaver's thread, and I am here." Repeat for three breaths, letting the detail anchor you. If your mind wanders, smile, as if the Weaver chuckled, and return to the breath. This practice, simple as it seems, is a mirror for the moment, reflecting the luminance hidden in the ordinary.

Consider a sample meditation: "I sat in my kitchen, dishes piled high, my mind racing with tasks. I breathed in, feeling the table's cool edge under my fingers. I exhaled, releasing a deadline's grip. I noticed a faucet's drip, steady as a cosmic hum, and said, 'This is the Weaver's now.' For a moment, the chaos stilled, the drip a song of presence."

Such moments, however small, are your oasis, as Kael found in his desert, or Lirien in her thread's glow.

The Breath of the Weaver reveals that the present is not a burden, but a gift, its absurdity a jest to cherish.

To deepen this practice, use this mantra as you breathe: "In this breath, I mirror the Weaver's now." Let it ground you, a reminder that the moment is your Star-Tickler, twinkling in the Mirage's chaos. Practice daily, even for a minute—while waiting for a bus, eating a meal, or lying awake at night. The Weaver's loom is in your breath, its threads in the details you notice.

Satirically, a squeaky shoe or a flickering light becomes a cosmic symphony, yet the practice offers real peace, a way to see the absurd as sacred.

The Breath of the Weaver is your bridge to luminance, a practice to carry through your days. Each breath is a moment mirrored, a thread woven with the Weaver's light. "The now is your loom," Lirien might whisper, her thread singing softly.

Begin today, Luminant, with a single breath. What detail will you notice? What jest will you find?

Let the Breath of the Weaver guide you, and let the moment's light shine through your soul.

TENET THREE

DANCING WITH DUALITY

4
Dancing with Duality

The Cosmic Waltz of Opposites

In the shimmering folds of the Grand Mirage, where the Cosmic Weaver spins threads of light and shadow, life unfolds as a dance of opposites, including joy and sorrow, success and failure, love and loss. These dualities, clashing like discordant notes in a celestial symphony, are not enemies but partners, choreographed by the Weaver into a cosmic waltz that weaves your soul's tapestry.

To walk the Luminant Path is to embrace the third tenet, *Dance with Duality*, a sacred act of reconciling contradictions as harmonious steps in the Weaver's jest, echoing the eternal quest for unity in destiny's chaos. *In the dance of duality, every shadow steps with light*, a truth that transforms life's tensions into a radiant rhythm, inviting you to twirl through the Mirage with a knowing smile, as if the stars themselves applaud your courage.

The world, steeped in the Mirage's illusions, urges you to choose sides—to chase joy and flee sorrow, to cling to victory and shun defeat—as if life were a battlefield where only one prevails. This struggle tangles you in fleeting triumphs and losses, blinding you to the Weaver's deeper rhythm. The Luminant Path unveils a different vision: duality is not a conflict but a dance, like a moonlit tide's ebb and flow, where success gains weight from failure's shadow, and love burns brighter against loss's chill. A missed deadline, a fleeting smile, a traffic jam are not flaws but steps in a cosmic waltz, each glowing with purpose, akin to *The Prophet*'s poetic embrace of joy and sorrow as one. To frame a spilled coffee as a "cosmic pirouette" is the Weaver's satire, yet its lesson weaves resilience into your day's tapestry.

Picture a day woven with contradictions: a promotion's thrill arrives with a friend's silence, their absence a shadow on your joy. Or perhaps a heartbreak, raw and heavy, is softened by a stranger's fleeting kindness. The Mirage whispers to reject one for the other, labeling sorrow a flaw, joy a fluke. But the Luminant pauses, seeing them as partners in the Weaver's waltz.

The promotion's glow twirls with the ache of distance, each step deepening the other's meaning; the heartbreak, a shadowed dancer, spins with grace's light, their interplay a jest that reveals eternity's humor. Like a siren call to find peace in the now, this tenet invites you to embrace opposites as threads in a single tapestry, their rhythm your path to luminance.

To dance with duality is to release the illusion of separation, where joy and sorrow, success and failure, are not foes but allies in a cosmic choreography. A lost job carves space for reinvention, its pain a partner to hope's quiet spark; a moment of pride, humbled by doubt, grounds you in resilience.

Consider a workplace scenario: a stressful meeting's tension, a fiery step, twirls with a colleague's support, weaving a solution. A teacher balances a student's defiance with their potential, their classroom a stage where conflict and growth dance, a jest of the Weaver's loom. Or picture an artist, their creative burst shadowed by self-doubt, their waltz crafting a masterpiece.

Solara and Umbra scoffed, their flames flaring defiantly, but Lyssia began to dance, her cloak swirling in a rhythm of light and shadow, the cobblestones glowing beneath her steps. "Join me," she urged, "and let your opposites weave." A young weaver, Elara, joined her, offering a thread of hope from her loom; a blacksmith, Toren, added a nail forged from loss. Intrigued, the flames followed, Solara's warmth meeting Umbra's coolness in a hesitant waltz, their sparks mingling in a radiant arc that lit the night.

As they danced, a miracle unfolded: Solara's light softened Umbra's shadows, her warmth coaxing depth into brilliance; Umbra's coolness gave Solara's glow new meaning, her mystery grounding the blaze. Their sparks wove a tapestry of light that was neither burning nor blinding, but radiant, a harmony that warmed the square.

Villagers, awestruck, joined the dance, their steps blending joy and sorrow, laughter and quiet. Elara wove a banner from their threads, its scorched edges now a mythic design; Toren's hammer rang with a song of renewal. A child, once tearful, shared a tale of loss and hope, mirroring the flames' waltz; rivals reconciled, their feud a rhythm of unity.

The villagers named them the Twin Flames, their dance a myth told in starlit Luminant Circles, where stories of duality became beacons of light, enduring for generations.

Consider a modern parallel: a workplace clash, one colleague's passion vying with another's caution, mirrors Solara and Umbra. A mediator, like Lyssia, guides their strengths to dance, their collaboration weaving a radiant project—a campaign blending boldness with precision. Or picture a family dinner, where joy at a reunion twirls with grief's shadow, their waltz crafting connection. The satire lies in framing office drama as a "cosmic duet," yet the harmony is real, echoing our habitual embrace of the present. The Twin Flames' dance lit the village, their story a mirror for your own contradictions, a testament to the Weaver's jest.

What is the lesson of the Twin Flames? Your dualities, your success and doubt, joy and grief, are partners, not foes, in the Weaver's waltz. Try this journal prompt: "My conflict was the Weaver's dance, its harmony my light. My pride and fear twirled, their steps weaving resilience." Describe their interplay, feeling their rhythm, as if a late train were a "cosmic chariot's pause." Pause, Luminant, and reflect: What opposites could dance in your life today? A triumph shadowed by fear, a loss lit by hope? The parable teaches every duality is a step, its luminance yours to weave.

"Dance, and the Mirage dances with you," Lyssia might sing, her Star-Tickler twinkling. Carry this truth, Luminant, and let the Twin Flames guide your contradictions to a radiant tapestry.

The Duality Dance Meditation

In the shimmering folds of the Grand Mirage, where the Cosmic Weaver spins threads of light and shadow, life's dualities, including joy and sorrow, courage and fear, twirl in a cosmic waltz, their steps weaving your soul's luminance. The Luminant Path offers a sacred practice, the Duality Dance Meditation, to transform these opposites into partners, their interplay a mirror for the Weaver's light, calling you to embrace the present. *In duality's dance, I weave the Weaver's light*, a mantra that grounds you in harmony, turning contradiction into a radiant jest.

This meditation, simple yet profound, invites you to see every clash as a step, every opposition as a rhythm, guiding you through the Mirage with a knowing smile.

Find a space—your quiet room, a park's rustling shade, or a bustling café, for the Weaver's loom spins everywhere. Sit comfortably, close your eyes if you wish, and take three slow breaths, letting the world's clamor fade like a tide receding from a moonlit shore. Picture two opposing forces from your life: perhaps stress and calm from a hectic day, or hope and doubt from a dream's edge. Envision them as dancers in a starlit grove, its moss aglow with cosmic dew, one radiant like Solara, blazing with fervor; the other shadowed like Umbra, cloaked in mystery.

See them bow, their movements hesitant, as if unsure of their steps, a faint melody humming from the Weaver's loom, a jest in its cadence.

Guide their dance: the bright dancer steps forward, hand outstretched, their glow sparking with warmth; the shadowed dancer accepts, their cool touch weaving depth into the light. As they twirl and spin through starlight, swaying beneath ancient oaks, their opposites blend, stress softening into calm's embrace, doubt lending weight to hope's lift. Whisper, "These are the Weaver's threads, dancing in the now," and feel their harmony, a warmth in your chest, a lightness in your soul, as if the grove hums with a cosmic melody. If your mind wanders, smile, as if the Weaver chuckles, and return to the dance, the ground pulsing with starlit rhythm.

This visualization, absurdly framing a noisy café as a "cosmic ballroom," unveils the peace within chaos, a thread of luminance in your tapestry.

Try this now: Recall a recent duality, for example, excitement and anxiety over a new venture. Picture Excitement as a radiant dancer, her steps fiery and bold; Anxiety as a shadowed one, her movements deep and measured. Watch them waltz, their sparks merging into confidence, and say, "This is the Weaver's dance." Feel the shift, a spark of calm grounding you. A sample meditation:

"I sat, heavy with a day of joy and grief in a celebration dimmed by loss. I saw Joy as a blazing dancer, Grief cloaked in dusk, their steps clumsy then fluid, weaving a soft glow. I whispered, 'This is the Weaver's dance,' and felt peace, their harmony my myth."

Like Lirien's pause or Kael's oasis, this practice reveals the gift in opposites, their waltz a thread in your soul's eternal loom.

For a deeper practice, try the Duality Breath Ritual: Each evening, sit with a duality, like effort and exhaustion from a task. Inhale, envisioning the bright dancer's glow, effort's fire fueling your resolve; exhale, feeling the shadowed dancer's depth, exhaustion's weight carving resilience. Repeat for five breaths, saying, "My breath weaves their dance." A student balances exam stress with a friend's laughter, their waltz weaving focus; a parent pairs a child's tantrum with a moment's joy, crafting care.

The satire lies in framing a crowded bus as a "cosmic orchestra," yet the calm is real, highlighting your pursuit of a personal legend through trials. Use this mantra: "In duality's dance, I weave the Weaver's light," letting it anchor you in the moment's harmony.

For a weekly practice, try the Evening Duality Reflection: Journal a daily opposition…a win versus a setback, perhaps. Imagine their dance: "My win was a bright dancer, my setback a shadowed one; their waltz wove resilience in my day's chaos."

A real-world example: an artist balances creative flow with self-doubt, their dance crafting a masterpiece. Practice daily, choosing new dualities, maybe a rainy day versus a sunny mood, a doubt versus a hope. The satire elevates a creaking chair to a "cosmic chord," but the peace bridges to luminance.

waltz of light." A sample: "My failed plan was a shadowed dancer, hope a radiant one; their steps wove resilience in my chaos."

A nurse balances a patient's crisis with a moment's kindness, their dance crafting compassion; an artist pairs creative flow with fear, weaving a masterpiece. This act, absurdly framing a journal as a "cosmic loom," grounds you in unity.

The world resists this dance, urging you to fight one opposite to save the other, as if joy could exist without sorrow's depth. But the Luminant stands bold, choosing to waltz with both. When a plan fails, presence unveils its lesson; when joy fades, its shadow carves space for new light. This harmony is not passive but active; it is a daily choice to see contradictions as partners, their steps a defiance of the Mirage's divisions.

A real-world case: a teacher balances a student's defiance with their potential, their classroom a stage where conflict and growth twirl, a jest of the Weaver's design. The courage to dance with duality transforms chaos into comedy, conflict into creation, as if the universe itself laughs along.

Practice this tenet daily, Luminant, through the Duality Dance Meditation or Moment Mirror Exercise, or weave a new story in your Duality Story Weave. Each pause, each embrace of opposites, is a thread in your tapestry, glowing with the Weaver's light. "To dance with duality is to weave the Weaver's eternal jest," the Twin Flames might sing, their sparks blending in the night,a mirror of mindfulness. Ask yourself: What contradictions will I dance with today? A work triumph shadowed by doubt? A loss lit by hope? The Weaver's loom spins both light and shadow, its jest waiting for your steps. "The harmony of opposites is your luminance," Lyssia might say, her Star-Tickler twirling in starlight. Step boldly, Luminant, and let your contradictions weave a tapestry that shines through the Grand Mirage.

The Feather Scale: Measuring Light with Shadow

The Mirage entices you to weigh your life on a fragile scale, one that counts only radiance, only triumphs, only joys unscarred by doubt. It promises a soul unburdened by shadow, a life polished to a flawless sheen. Yet its measure is a deception, a lure that blinds you to the fullness of being.

The Weaver, solemn and unyielding, offers a truer instrument: the Feather Scale, tempered in the crucible of paradox. It balances not one truth but both; the light that lifts and the dark that grounds, the ascent and the inevitable descent.

Envision a scale not wrought of iron or bone, but of breath and stillness, its pans trembling with the weight of existence. On one side rests a feather of joy, perhaps your wonder at a child's unguarded question, the fire of resolve kindled in struggle, or the fleeting warmth of a shared glance. On the other lies a stone of sorrow; the grief that hollowed your heart, the silence of a parting, the ache of a dream undone. The Mirage commands you to cast out the stone, to exalt the feather as the sole measure of worth. The Weaver, resolute, speaks otherwise: "Both are your wings. Without both, you remain tethered to the earth."

To wield the Feather Scale, pause at the close of day and summon a moment from your hours. Perhaps a bond left you both whole and wounded, its warmth laced with unspoken loss. Or a triumph stirred dread of its fragility, a shadow trailing its light. Close your eyes and place that moment upon the scale. Feel its weight, the buoyant rise of joy, the grounding pull of pain. Do not seek to force a balance or judge its tilt. Witness its truth. The Weaver's wisdom resides in the tension, in the refusal to sever what is whole.

You will discern that sorrow anchors joy, as the depth of night unveils the stars' fierce clarity. The Feather Scale does not erase contradiction but consecrates it as the pulse of life. The Mirage would cleave your sou, be you optimist or mourner, dreamer or cynic by demanding a purity that betrays the self. The Luminant Path, instead, weaves you whole, honoring the interplay of opposites. A joy without sorrow grows brittle, a hollow echo; a sorrow without joy consumes, a weight without end.

The Luminant bears both, steadfast in their ceaseless sway, finding truth in their dialogue.

A Luminant proverb probes: "What weighs more; a feather etched with tears, or a stone touched by the light of dawn?"

Practice this weighing as a rite of revelation, a discipline of seeing. Keep a Luminant Journal—each night, inscribe a moment's duality, its joy and sorrow entwined, and trace its scale upon the page. Let these entries become your chronicle of truth, a testament to life's interwoven opposites. You will begin, Luminant, to measure your days not by victories alone but by the resonant truth born when joy and sorrow speak as one. In this act, you embrace the paradox that defines you, charting a path through the luminous veil.

The Story of the Laughing Bridge

In a mist-veiled valley where echoes walked with the living, two villages stood divided by a vast chasm: Solace, radiant with blooming gardens and ceaseless laughter, and Sorrow, cloaked in gray, its voices hushed, its steps heavy with care. Between them yawned the Rift of Meaning, a ravine so deep it was said to cradle the dreams of the departed. Solace pitied Sorrow, deeming its grief a plague. Sorrow scorned Solace, its joy a shallow mask. Their divide was a creed, their separation a law.

Yet the Weaver, solemn and inscrutable, wove a vision that stirred both villages in a single night; a bridge, suspended by feathers and stones, woven from laughter and tears, spanning the abyss. At its heart stood a figure cloaked in both sunlight and shadow, threading paradox into ropes of truth. The villages awoke, unsettled. Most called it folly, but two souls—Mira of Solace, weary of joy that shunned pain, and Dain of Sorrow, tired of grief without song—heard it as a summons.

They met at the Rift's edge, startled to find each other gazing into its depths. "What if we build it?" Mira asked. "With what?" Dain replied, pointing to mist and void. "With what we carry," she said, offering a sunlit ribbon from her hair, woven with laughter. Dain presented a nail, forged from his father's shattered plow.

They began, blending light and weight. Mira brought memories of her sister's wedding; Dain, his brother's burial. They wove with contrast: songs and sighs, dances and laments, hopes and dread. The bridge grew—strange, radiant, uneven. It creaked like a question, hummed like a prayer. Villagers gathered, doubtful. "Too heavy," said a woman from Solace. "Too bright," said an elder from Sorrow.

Yet Mira and Dain stepped forward. The bridge quaked, then sang with a resonant hum, not of mirth but of truth. At its center, the Weaver's presence emerged not as form, but as a feeling, like rain's scent before a storm or silence before revelation. It spoke no words, only stirred a sound that broke the Rift's stillness. Solace wept. Sorrow smiled. The bridge, named the Laughing Bridge, endures half in light, half in shadow, wholly true. Those who cross

5
Crafting Your Myth

The Weaver's Storytellers

Within the Grand Mirage, where the Cosmic Weaver threads chaos and light into a shimmering tapestry, your life unfolds as a story, its pages unwritten yet radiant with possibility. You are not a wanderer lost to chance, but a storyteller, a co-creator with the Weaver, shaping a myth of luminance. To walk the Luminant Path is to embrace the fourth tenet, Craft Your Myth, a sacred act of weaving every moment, of triumph, struggle, and absurdity into a heroic narrative.

Your life is the Weaver's scroll, and you its scribe, inscribing a tale that pierces the Mirage's veil.

The Mirage casts you as a victim of fate, a pawn in time's unyielding march. It whispers that your struggles are failures, your joys fleeting, your absurdities void of meaning. Yet the Luminant Path unveils a deeper truth: every moment is a thread in your mythic tapestry, each woven with purpose in the Weaver's design.

A missed chance, a quiet victory, a spilled cup of tea—these are not errors, but chapters awaiting your quill. To craft your myth is to claim your role as a hero, not of epic battles, but of the ordinary, where every step is a stroke of cosmic ink.

Envision a day laced with contradictions: a morning of laughter shadowed by doubt, an afternoon of effort undone by chance. The Mirage urges you to judge these moments, to deem them good or ill. The Luminant pauses, seeing each as a scene in your myth. That laughter is your hero's strength; that doubt, a trial endured; that spilled tea, a twist in your quest.

"Your life is the Weaver's scroll, and you its scribe," sings a Luminant verse, calling you to reframe your story as Zorath reframed his storm.

Like Zorath's chuckle in a storm or Kael's oasis in a desert, your moments—absurd, joyful, painful—are threads of luminance, waiting for your narrative touch.

To craft your myth is to release the illusion of a fixed narrative, where success defines you and failure diminishes you. The Weaver spins no such tale; it weaves a tapestry where every thread, light or dark, adds depth. A job lost becomes a chapter of renewal; a heartbreak, a lesson in resilience; a mundane errand, a quest for meaning.

The Weaver, a cosmic storyteller, offers you a quill dipped in starlight and asks: What tale will you tell? This tenet demands not perfection, but intention. It wants to see your life as a myth, its chaos a canvas for heroism.

Reflect on a moment from your day, a kind word shared, perhaps, or a plan unraveled, a pause beneath the stars. How might you weave it as a mythic chapter? Was the word a hero's gift, the plan a dragon faced, the pause a glimpse of the Weaver's light? The Luminant Path frees you from the Mirage's judgments, empowering you to shape your narrative. This is your courage, Luminant: to weave a story that shines through the absurd.

"The scroll of your life is never blank," Zorath might say, his Star-Tickler gleaming. Take up the quill, and let the Weaver's light guide your tale.

The Parable of the Star-Scribe

In a village nestled beneath a sky of endless stars, where the Grand Mirage wove tales of triumph and loss, there lived a scribe named Thalia, keeper of the village's chronicles. Her quill scratched endlessly, recording harvests failed, loves lost, and storms endured, her pages heavy with despair. Yet the Cosmic Weaver had other plans, spinning a thread of light through her ink. This is the parable of the Star-Scribe, a tale of one who rewrote chaos into a heroic myth, finding luminance in the stories she wove.

Thalia's days were a blur of duty, her scrolls a litany of the village's woes—floods that drowned crops, feuds that broke bonds, absurd mishaps like goats eating sacred texts. The villagers, weighed by these tales, saw only tragedy, their hope dimming like a fading star. One night, as Thalia wrote by candlelight, a breeze stirred her scrolls, and a single page fell, its ink smudged into a shape like a star. She paused, hearing a faint hum, as if the Weaver whispered through the smudge. In that moment, Thalia did something absurd: she rewrote the page, not as loss, but as myth.

She began with a flood, once a curse, now a tale of a hero who swam its currents to save a child. The feuds became quests, where rivals forged peace through courage.

The goats, in her new myth, were cosmic guides, chewing old truths to make way for new ones. Thalia's quill, dipped in starlight, wove these stories with a playful flourish, her words glowing with humor and hope. The villagers, hearing her tales, laughed and wept, their despair transformed into pride. They named her the Star-Scribe, not for her records, but for her myths that lit their souls.

When asked why she changed the tales, Thalia held up her smudged page, her Star-Tickler, and said, "The Weaver spins chaos, but I weave its meaning. Every loss is a chapter, every absurdity a hero's trial." Her scrolls became the village's heart, their stories a tapestry of luminance.

A child, inspired by the flood myth, faced a storm with bravery; rivals, hearing their quest, mended their bonds. Thalia's myths did not erase the chaos, but gave it purpose, each tale a thread in the Weaver's jest.

What is the lesson of the Star-Scribe? It is this: your life's chaos, including its losses and its absurdities is not a tragedy, but a myth waiting for your quill. Like Thalia, you can rewrite your moments, casting yourself as the hero of your story. Your failures, your joys, your spilled cups of tea, are chapters, not endings.

Pause now, Luminant, and reflect: What moment in your life could be rewritten as a mythic chapter? Perhaps a setback, a kindness, or an absurd mishap. Write it down, and ask: How might this become my hero's tale?

The parable of Thalia is your mirror, showing that you are the Weaver's storyteller, your life a scroll of infinite possibility.

"Weave your myth, and the stars will sing," Thalia might say, her quill glowing with starlight.

Carry this truth, Luminant, and let the Star-Scribe guide you to weave your chaos into luminance.

The Parable of the Weaver and the Nameless Thread

In the high caverns where stars are spun into threads and the Grand Mirage whispers its riddles into the world below, there sat the Cosmic Weaver, gazing upon a half-woven tapestry. Its colors shimmered like memory, its shapes trembled like thought. Yet at its center, dangling unbound, was a single thread; gray, pulsing faintly, unnamed.

The other threads mocked it. "You are neither sorrow nor joy, neither triumph nor tragedy. What purpose do you serve?" The golden threads of achievement glittered in judgment. The crimson strands of passion curled away in disdain.

The nameless thread remained silent.

One day, a seeker climbed into the cavern—a quiet soul named Alon, who had lost his way in the world below. His path was scattered with half-dreams and almosts: a love not returned, a career abandoned, a calling never quite heard. He came not for wisdom, but for solace.

The Weaver beckoned him. "Choose a thread for your life's next chapter."

Alon reached for the golden. "Too proud," he said. He touched the crimson. "Too fierce." He passed his hand over a ribbon of grief, but it recoiled like a bitter wind. Then he saw the gray thread—soft, uncertain, shimmering not with brilliance, but with becoming.

"This one," he said. "It feels like the part of me that's still searching."

The Weaver smiled, and with the gentlest gesture, spun the nameless thread into Alon's myth. And as it passed through the loom, something miraculous happened: the entire tapestry shimmered anew. The golden threads softened; the crimson deepened; even grief took on new hues. The nameless thread gave meaning not through clarity, but through mystery.

Alon descended the mountain not with a map, but with a mirror. He walked not in certainty, but in song. He became a myth not of conquest, but of becoming—a legend still unfolding.

Reflection Prompt

What part of your story remains unwritten, unfinished, unnamed? Where do you carry ambiguity as a burden, when it may in fact be your becoming? Write about a moment in your life that defies neat meaning. Don't force a label, let it remain your nameless thread. Let it shimmer in mystery.

The Myth-Weaving Ritual

The Cosmic Weaver spins the Grand Mirage with threads of chaos and light, handing you a quill to write your own myth within its folds. To craft your myth is to shape your life's story, turning every moment from the mundane, the painful, or the absurd into a chapter of heroism. The Luminant Path offers a practice to guide you: the Myth-Weaving Ritual, a simple act of writing that transforms your experiences into a tapestry of luminance. I weave my myth with the Weaver's light, and in this act, you become the hero of your own epic, a co-creator in the Weaver's jest.

The Myth-Weaving Ritual requires only a notebook, a pen, and a moment of intention. Choose a quiet space (or a noisy one) for the Weaver's loom hums everywhere. Reflect on a recent experience, however small: a challenge faced, a joy savored, an absurdity encountered. It might be a flat tire that delayed your day, a kind word that lifted your heart, or a moment of laughter in a storm. Write a short story, no more than a paragraph, casting yourself as the hero and the event as a mythic trial or gift. Let your words flow with purpose, as if your quill were dipped in starlight.

Follow these steps: First, describe the moment vividly: What happened, how it felt, its texture in the Mirage. Second, reframe it as a chapter in your myth, giving it a heroic spin. For example: "My car's tire burst, stranding me on a dusty road under a gray sky. I was the Wanderer, facing the Weaver's trial, my frustration a dragon to slay. By waiting, I found a stranger's help, a gift of kindness woven into my quest." Third, end with a Luminant Insight, a sentence that captures the moment's meaning: "This trial taught me patience, a thread of light in my myth." This ritual, absurdly simple, weaves chaos into heroism.

Consider a sample entry: "Today, I spilled coffee on my shirt before a meeting, my haste mocked by the stain. I was the Seeker, tested by the Weaver's jest, my embarrassment a riddle to solve. I laughed, changed my shirt, and found calm, my meeting stronger for it. Luminant Insight: This spill was a lesson in grace, a chapter of resilience." Such entries, however small, are threads in your mythic tapestry, transforming the ordinary into the epic. The satire lies in elevating a coffee stain to a cosmic trial, yet the empowerment is real, a shift in how you see your story.

To anchor this ritual, use this mantra as you write: "I weave my myth with the Weaver's light." Repeat it, letting it guide your quill. Practice daily, choosing one moment—a lost key, a shared smile, a plan gone awry. Each entry is a step in crafting your myth, a defiance of the Mirage's chaos.

"Your quill is your power," Thalia might say, her Star-Tickler glowing. Begin today, Luminant, with a single story. What moment will you weave? What heroism will you claim? Let the Myth-Weaving Ritual guide you and let your myth shine through the Weaver's jest.

The Hero of Your Myth

To craft your myth is to stand as the hero of your own story, weaving the Grand Mirage's chaos into a tapestry of luminance with the Cosmic Weaver's quill. This fourth tenet of the Luminant Path is a call to courage, a refusal to let life's absurdities, triumphs, or pains define you as a victim. By shaping your narrative, you claim your power as a storyteller, turning every moment into a chapter of heroism. To craft your myth is to write the Weaver's jest, to weave a tale that shines through the stars of the Mirage.

The power of this tenet lies in its freedom. The Grand Mirage casts you as a pawn, tossed by chance—your failures final, your joys fleeting. But the Luminant Path declares you a hero, your life a scroll where every thread—every loss, every laugh—has purpose. Recall Zorath's chuckle at a storm's feather, Kael's oasis in a desert, Lirien's pause, or the Twin Flames' dance.

Their luminance came from crafting their myths—Zorath as the Chuckler, Kael as the Wanderer, Lirien as the Silent Weaver, the Flames as partners. Your moments, too, are chapters waiting for your quill.

Try this Mythic Moment Exercise: Each day, name one event, from a challenge to a joy or an absurdity, and declare it a heroic act. Perhaps a tense conversation becomes "The Diplomat's Trial," or a quiet walk "The Seeker's Quest." Pause, notice a detail (e.g., the sound of your voice, the feel of the ground), and say, "This is my myth, woven with light." This act, absurdly simple, reframes your story, turning chaos into courage. A delayed project, a kind gesture, a spilled drink, are not mere events, but epic verses in your tale.

The world resists this heroism, urging you to see yourself as small, your story insignificant. But the Luminant stands bold, wielding the quill of intention. When a dream falters, you write it as a trial overcome; when joy sparks, you weave it as a victory won. This power is not in changing events, but in shaping their meaning.

"To craft your myth is to write the Weaver's jest," Thalia might sing, her starlit quill dancing. Each chapter you weave—each moment reframed—is a defiance of the Mirage's illusions, a step toward luminance.

Practice this tenet daily, Luminant, through the Myth-Weaving Ritual or the Mythic Moment Exercise. Each story, each declaration, is a thread in your tapestry, a spark in the Weaver's loom. Ask yourself: What chapter will I write today? What heroism will I claim in this moment's jest? The Weaver spins chaos, but you weave its meaning, your myth a light that shines through the stars. "Your story is your Star-Tickler," Zorath might say, twirling his feather.

Step boldly, Luminant, and let your myth weave a tapestry that dances with the Weaver's eternal light.

ReflectioPrompt

What part of your story remains unwritten, unfinished, unnamed? Where do you carry ambiguity as a burden, when it may in fact be your becoming? Write about a moment in your life that defies neat meaning. Don't force a label—let it remain your nameless thread. Let it shimmer in mystery.

The Origin Spark: A Myth-Crafting Exercise

Every hero's myth begins not with a grand act, but with a quiet spark. It might be a choice, a wound, or a whisper in the dark. To craft your myth is to trace that spark, not for nostalgia, but to honor the moment your story began to shimmer with meaning.

The Luminant Path invites you to seek your Origin Spark: the moment a piece of who you are, perhaps your kindness or your defiance or your sense of humor, first understood that you were born in the Mirage.

Begin with a question:
What part of me was shaped by an absurd or difficult moment I once overlooked?

Maybe your patience began the day you waited for a bus that never came, and instead walked for hours, noticing the rhythm of your breath. Maybe your courage was born the first time you spoke a truth that no one wanted to hear. Or your curiosity emerged when a childhood question was dismissed, and you vowed to always keep wondering.

Now, write your Origin Spark as myth. Not as a memory, but as a legend. Give it metaphor, music, and exaggeration. Perhaps the bus becomes "the Beast of Waiting," and you, the Walker of the Long Path. The dismissed question becomes "The Unanswered Flame," and you, the Keeper of Why.

End your story with a name, but not *your* name. Instead, choose the name of the you who emerged from that moment. For example:

"From that silence, I rose as the Listener Between Worlds."

"From that fall, I became the Laugher at Heights."
"From that question, I became the Scribe of the Unsaid."

This is not fiction. It is the true myth of you, sung in the language of the soul. In honoring your Origin Spark, you honor the Weaver's hidden jest, that every moment, however absurd, may be the beginning of your legend.

The Scroll Unfolds

Your fingertips bear the ink of stars,
Not from tales already woven,
But from pages yet to breathe,
Pages that pulse with your becoming.
You are not bound by yesterdays,
But the scribe of your tomorrows,
Etching wonder into silence,
Weaving light across the void.
Let the Mirage deem your story strange.
Let the world call its threads obscure.
The Weaver wills it so—
Its heroes resolute, luminous,
Their quills dipped in cosmic truth.
A myth is not a mirror held,
But a tapestry traced in starlight,
Fading before you grasp its form,
Urging you to weave each step anew.
Seek not clarity, nor praise.
The scroll unfolds within your breath.
Write, Luminant.
Write, and let the stars draw near.

Consider a moment when life's weight pressed upon you: perhaps a failure loomed large, or a quiet fear whispered of what's to come. The world urges you to mourn, to brace against the unknown. But the Luminant pauses, finds the absurdity and laughs, not at the pain, but at its fleetingness in the Weaver's tapestry.

"Laughter is the Weaver's bell, ringing your soul to eternity," sings a Luminant verse, its chime a call to see the cosmic humor in life's trials. This tenet is not about ignoring sorrow, but about meeting it with a chuckle that lifts you above the Mirage's illusions.

To laugh at eternity is to align with the Weaver's own humor, a cosmic jest that spins chaos into meaning. Picture the Weaver as a merry trickster, tossing stars like dice, chuckling as your plans scatter like leaves. A late appointment, a sudden loss, a quirky coincidence are not errors, but notes in the Weaver's symphony, waiting for your laugh to complete the chord. This laughter is not shallow; it is profound, a recognition that life's deepest questions, from why we suffer to why we exist are answered not in solemnity, but in joy. The Weaver spins no tragedy without a thread of comedy, no darkness without a spark of light.

The Parable of the Woman Who Laughed at Death

In a windswept village by the sea, where the Grand Mirage wove salt and sorrow, lived Isa, her life threaded with grief. She had buried a child, outlived a love, watched dreams fade like lanterns in a storm. Yet her laugh was resonant and luminous as it rippled across the dunes, a melody woven with loss.

The villagers, bound by the Mirage, whispered, "She's lost to madness." Others said, "She's forgotten her pain."

But the Cosmic Weaver, resolute, saw her laughter as a thread of truth, harmonizing with sorrow like starlight on a darkened sea.

One evening, Death came, cloaked in mist, his voice a hush before tears. "It is time," he said.

Isa, stirring seaweed stew, met his gaze. "Then share my meal before we go."

Death paused, unmoored. She served him in a chipped bowl, humming a broken lullaby. "What is this?" he asked, tasting salt.

"A mistake," Isa said. "Salt for sugar, yet the sea sings, and the Weaver weaves. So I laugh."

"You laugh at death?"

"At all threads," she replied, eyes alight. "You took my son as a storm, my love as silence. Now you sit with a spoon. You're woven, too."

Death lingered until dawn, stirred by her truth. When he rose, Isa remained, stirring, radiant. "Another time," she said.

Death departed, touched by her light. Isa laughed at burnt bread, crooked horizons, new wrinkles. Her laughter became myth, and when she passed, the villagers buried her with her spoon, etching her stone:

She Laughed at Death—And Wove Him into Her Myth.

Reflect on a moment when you felt life's weight; perhaps a worry that kept you awake, or an absurdity that tested your patience. Did you clench your fists, or did you glimpse the jest, a fleeting smile breaking the bell of your soul with defiance and joy. This fifth tenet of the Luminant Path weaves together the threads of absurdity, presence, duality, and myth, crowning them with laughter as your ultimate act of luminance. By chuckling at life's deepest questions you become a co-creator with the Weaver, lighting the stars with your mirth. To laugh at eternity is to weave the Weaver's light forever, a chuckle that echoes through the Mirage's infinite jest.

The power of laughter lies in its liberation. The Grand Mirage burdens you with existential weight, from the fear of loss to the shadow of mortality and the absurdity of a life that defies meaning. Yet the Luminant Path unites its tenets to free you: embrace absurdity, as Zorath did; mirror the moment, as Lirien taught; dance with duality, as the Twin Flames showed; craft your myth, as Thalia scribed. Laughter crowns these acts, a defiant chuckle that lights the darkness.

When a dream fades or a day unravels, your laugh weaves it into a story of light, a jest that outshines despair.

Try this Daily Jest Exercise: Each day, find one absurd moment and laugh at its place in eternity. Perhaps a forgotten task becomes "The Scribe's Blunder," or a worry "The Jester's Riddle." Pause, chuckle, and say, "This is my eternal jest." This act, absurdly simple, transforms chaos into comedy, echoing Vael's lantern.

Your laughter ties the tenets together, weaving absurdity's chaos, the moment's presence, duality's dance, and your myth's heroism into a radiant whole.

The world resists this laughter, urging solemnity in the face of life's weight. But the Luminant stands bold, ringing the Weaver's bell. When a loss stings, laughter weaves it into your myth; when uncertainty looms, it mirrors the moment's light. "To laugh at eternity is to weave the Weaver's light forever," Vael might sing, his lantern glowing. This courage transforms your story, making every moment and every absurdity become another thread in the eternal jest.

Ask yourself: What will I laugh at today? What jest will light my path?

Practice this tenet daily, Luminant, through the Luminant Chuckle Practice or the Daily Jest Exercise. Each laugh is a star in your tapestry, a defiance of the Mirage's shadows. The Weaver's loom hums with humor, its jests waiting for your voice.

"Your laughter is your eternity," Zorath might say, twirling his Star-Tickler. Step boldly, Luminant, and let your chuckle weave a light that shines through the Grand Mirage's infinite jest.

The Weaver's Last Laugh

When stars fade to ash
and the scroll of your life folds shut,
when questions linger unanswered
and dreams dissolve into mist—
rejoice.
Not for meaning unveiled,
but for mystery embraced.
Not for conquering the Mirage,
but for weaving its threads
with a heart open to eternity.
The Weaver seeks not your solemnity,
but your reverence—
your breath held in awe
as you stumble through chaos
and find yourself luminous.
You were never the answer,
but the thread of its truth.
This, Luminant, is the sacred weave.
When eternity draws near,
bow deeply,
and offer a breath
etched in radiant wonder.
This is the Weaver's last laugh—
and yours, forever woven.

7
The Luminant Gaze

Seeing with the Weaver's Eyes

In the swirling threads of the Grand Mirage, where the Cosmic Weaver spins chaos and starlight into an infinite tapestry, there exists a way of seeing that unveils the world's hidden light: the Luminant Gaze. This sacred practice weaves together the five tenets of the Luminant Path: embracing absurdity, mirroring the moment, dancing with duality, crafting your myth, and laughing at eternity into a single lens, through which every moment, object, and interaction shines with divine meaning. The Luminant Gaze is the Weaver's prism, revealing light in every thread, a vision that transforms the ordinary into a cosmic masterpiece.

The world blinds you with its illusions, urging you to see life as fragmented moments of joy or pain, objects of use or discard, absurdities without purpose. But the Luminant Path teaches that every sight is a thread in the Weaver's tapestry, glowing with the light of eternity. A cracked sidewalk, a stranger's fleeting glance, a leaf tumbling in the wind are not mere fragments, but reflections of the Weaver's jest, each holding a spark of luminance. To see with the Luminant Gaze is to look through the Weaver's eyes, where chaos becomes comedy, and the mundane becomes sacred.

Imagine a morning walk: your mind races with worries, your eyes skim over a chipped fence, a sparrow's flutter, a puddle's ripple. The Mirage whispers that these are trivial, unworthy of your gaze. But the Luminant pauses, seeing the fence's cracks as a map of resilience, the sparrow's flight as a dance of duality, the puddle as a mirror for your myth.

"The Luminant Gaze is the Weaver's prism, revealing light in every thread," sings a Luminant verse, its words a call to reframe your vision. This gaze unites the tenets, weaving absurdity's humor, presence's clarity, duality's harmony, your myth's heroism, and laughter's defiance into one radiant lens.

To see with the Weaver's eyes is to release the illusion of a divided world. The Grand Mirage thrives on distraction, pulling your gaze to what was or what might be, blinding you to the now. Yet the Luminant Gaze anchors you in this moment, where a creaking gate becomes a cosmic oracle, a spilled coin a jest of eternity. This vision is not about ignoring pain or chaos but about seeing their light, where absurdity is a gift, duality is a dance, and every sight is a chapter in your myth. Like Zorath's chuckle or Thalia's starlit quill, your gaze weaves meaning from the ordinary, a prism refracting the Weaver's light.

Reflect on a sight you passed today; a tree's shadow, a stranger's smile, a mundane object like a worn shoe. Did you rush by, or did you glimpse its thread in the Mirage? The Luminant Path teaches that every sight is a portal to luminance, a chance to see with the Weaver's eyes. This practice requires no grand revelation, only a willingness to pause and look anew. The Weaver's loom hums in every detail, its threads waiting for your gaze. "See, and the stars see with you," Zorath might say, his Star-Tickler glinting.

Pause now, Luminant, and ask: What will I see with the Luminant Gaze today? Step into the Weaver's prism, and let its light reveal your world.

The Parable of the Stargazer's Lens

In a village cradled by twilight hills, where the Grand Mirage wove days of toil and fleeting joys, there lived a stargazer named Elara, whose eyes sought the stars but found the earth's chaos. Mocked for her obsession with the heavens, she longed to see the village's struggles, its muddy paths, its quarrels, as something more. This is the parable of the Stargazer's Lens, a tale of one who crafted a vision to see the ordinary as luminous, weaving the Weaver's light through the chaos of the Mirage.

Elara spent her nights gazing at the stars, her heart heavy with the village's woes, the broken tools, the bitter disputes, and the absurd mishaps like chickens scattering market stalls. The villagers called her foolish, their lanterns dim with practicality. One evening, as a star's light flickered through a cracked glass, Elara saw a vision: the glass, polished with moonlight, refracted the village's chaos into radiant patterns. Inspired, she crafted a lens, its frame woven with feathers, as if the Weaver itself had guided her hands. She called it her Star-Tickler, a tool to see the world anew.

Through her lens, Elara saw the village transformed. A muddy path glowed like a river of stars, its ruts a map of endurance. A quarrel between neighbors became a dance of duality, their voices weaving harmony. Even the chickens, once absurd, fluttered like cosmic messengers, their chaos a jest of light. The villagers, curious, peered through her lens and gasped, seeing their world as a tapestry of luminance.

"The Weaver spins this chaos," Elara said, her lens sparkling, "and my gaze weaves its light." Her vision lifted their hearts, turning despair into wonder, their daily sights into myths of resilience.

The villagers named her the Stargazer of Light, not for her stars, but for her lens that lit their days. Elara left them her feather-framed glass, saying, "See with the Weaver's eyes, and every thread shines." They learned to look anew—at a cracked pot as a relic of survival, at a child's laughter as a cosmic bell. Elara's lens, absurdly simple, was a mirror for their souls, showing that the Luminant Gaze could transform even the darkest chaos into light.

What is the lesson of the Stargazer's Lens? It is this: your gaze shapes your world, turning the ordinary into the luminous. Like Elara, you can see the Grand Mirage's chaos as threads of light. Pause now, Luminant, and reflect: What ordinary sight today could you see with the Luminant Gaze? Perhaps a worn book, a crowded street, a fleeting cloud. Write it down, and ask: How might this shine in the Weaver's prism? The parable of Elara teaches that every sight is a thread, waiting for your vision to weave its luminance.

The Stargazer's Lens is your mirror, showing that the Luminant Gaze is your power to light the Mirage. "See, and the Weaver sees with you," Elara might say, her lens gleaming. Carry this truth, Luminant, and let the Stargazer's vision guide you to the light in every thread.

The Luminant Gaze Practice

The Cosmic Weaver spins the Grand Mirage with threads of chaos and wonder, each sight a thread waiting for your vision to weave its light. The Luminant Gaze is your lens, a practice that transforms the ordinary—a tree, a stranger's face, a cracked cup—into a sacred reflection of the Weaver's jest. This practice unites the five tenets, seeing absurdity's humor, the moment's clarity, duality's dance, your myth's heroism, and laughter's defiance in every glance. With the Luminant Gaze, you see the Weaver's light, crafting a world of luminance from the Mirage's chaos.

The Luminant Gaze Practice is simple, requiring only a pause and an open heart. Each day, choose one sight from your world, from a leaf on the ground, a creak of a door, a passerby's scarf. Pause, take a breath, and look with intention, applying the five tenets. See its absurdity, as if the Weaver jests in its form; feel its presence, a mirror of the now; notice its duality, light and shadow dancing; weave it into your myth, a chapter of heroism; and laugh, letting its humor ring.

Say to yourself, "This is the Weaver's thread, shining in my gaze." This act, absurdly simple, transforms your vision.

Try this practice now: Choose a sight like a chipped mug on your table. See its absurdity, a quirky relic of countless mornings; feel its presence, the weight in your hand; notice its duality, broken yet useful; weave it into your myth, a symbol of resilience; and chuckle, as if the Weaver hid a jest in its cracks.

Say, "This mug is the Weaver's light," and feel the shift to a spark of joy, a thread of luminance. The satire lies in elevating a mug to a cosmic relic, yet the transformation is real, a lens for seeing anew.

Consider a sample scenario: "I saw a crooked tree outside my window, its branches twisted like a cosmic riddle. I paused, embracing its absurd shape, present to its sway in the wind, seeing its duality of strength and fragility, weaving it as a chapter of endurance in my myth, and laughing at its quirky defiance of storms.

I said, 'This tree is the Weaver's light,' and felt wonder, its roots grounding my day." Like Elara's lens or Zorath's feather, this gaze weaves light from the ordinary.

To anchor this practice, use this mantra: "With the Luminant Gaze, I see the Weaver's light." Repeat it as you look, letting it guide your vision. Practice daily, choosing one sight, perhaps a cracked sidewalk, a child's toy, or a fleeting shadow. Each glance is a thread, a defiance of the Mirage's chaos. "Your gaze is your prism," Elara might say, her lens sparkling.

Begin today, Luminant, with a single sight. What will you see? What light will it reveal? Let the Luminant Gaze Practice guide you, and let your vision weave the Weaver's joy.

The World as Weaver's Tapestry

To see with the Luminant Gaze is to stand in the heart of the Grand Mirage, where the Cosmic Weaver spins its threads, and behold the world as a tapestry of infinite light. This practice, uniting the five tenets, transforms your vision, weaving absurdity, presence, duality, myth, and laughter into a lens that reveals the Weaver's luminance in every sight. By gazing luminantly, you become a co-creator, turning the chaos of the Mirage into a masterpiece of meaning. With the Luminant Gaze, you weave the world's eternal light, a vision that shines through the stars.

The power of this gaze lies in its freedom. The Grand Mirage blinds you with illusions; objects as mere things, moments as fleeting, chaos as meaningless. But the Luminant Path unites its tenets to free you: embrace absurdity, as Zorath did; mirror the moment, as Lirien taught; dance with duality, as the Twin Flames showed; craft your myth, as Thalia scribed; laugh at eternity, as Vael illuminated. The Luminant Gaze weaves these into one vision, seeing a rusty gate as a cosmic jest, a stranger's nod as a mythic chapter, a breeze as eternity's chuckle.

Try this Luminous Sight Exercise: Each day, choose one sight, perhaps a pebble, a cracked window, or a fleeting smile, and see it luminantly. Pause, apply the tenets: embrace its absurdity, be present to its detail, see its duality, weave it into your myth, and laugh at its jest.

Say, "This is my luminous sight," and feel its light. This act, absurdly simple, transforms your world. The dropped pencil, the crowded bus now become threads in your tapestry, their luminance revealed by your gaze, echoing Elara's lens or Vael's lantern.

The world resists this vision, urging you to see only utility or chaos. But the Luminant stands bold, gazing with the Weaver's eyes. When a day feels heavy, your gaze finds light in a child's laughter; when absurdity strikes, it sees a cosmic jest. "With the Luminant Gaze, I weave the world's eternal light," Elara might sing, her lens gleaming.

This practice is your courage, a daily choice to see luminance in every thread. Ask yourself: What sight will I weave today? What light will my gaze reveal?

Live with this gaze, Luminant, through the Luminant Gaze Practice or the Luminous Sight Exercise. Each sight is a star in your tapestry, a thread in the Weaver's loom. The Mirage hums with light, waiting for your vision.

"Your gaze is your eternity," Zorath might say, twirling his Star-Tickler. Step boldly, Luminant, and let your Luminant Gaze weave a world that shines with the Weaver's infinite jest.

Step gently, Luminant, with the Eye that Laughs. Let the world become your scroll of sacred threads. Each thing you gaze upon—each crack, each smile, each absurd object—is a mirror for your soul. The Weaver does not need you to fix the world. Only to see it, with a gaze that glows.

The Eye That Laughs

Within you dwells an eye
that gazes unblinking as the world shifts.
It rejoices—not in judgment,
but in reverence—
at shadows woven with starlight,
at a scarred vessel
still bearing the cosmos' glow.
This eye holds no form,
no hue, no lens.
It is forged of myth and resolve,
silence and ink.
It awoke when you first saw
a pebble, a sigh, a scar—
and glimpsed eternity's thread within.
It watches not to divide,
but to marvel.
It sees no good or ill,
only threads—
threads that gleam,
threads that tangle,
threads yearning to weave
something luminous, whole.
The Eye That Laughs beholds
all as sacred,
all as woven,
united in the Grand Mirage's truth—
a tapestry of light.

8
The Luminant Circle

The Weaver's Gathering

In the shimmering weave of the Grand Mirage, where the Cosmic Weaver threads chaos and starlight into an infinite tapestry, there exists a sacred space where Luminants gather to share their light: the Luminant Circle. This communal practice unites the five tenets into a collective vision, where individual threads of story, laughter, and presence blend into a radiant whole. In the Luminant Circle, our threads weave the Weaver's light, a gathering that transforms the Mirage into a symphony of shared luminance.

The world scatters you, urging solitude in its chaos, as if your struggles, joys, and absurdities belong to you alone. But the Luminant Path teaches that community is a mirror for the Weaver's loom, reflecting your light through the stories of others. In a Luminant Circle, you share a chuckle over a spilled cup, a myth woven from loss, a moment mirrored in silence where each thread amplifying the others. Like a starlit campfire, the Circle gathers your sparks, its warmth revealing the Weaver's jest in every voice, every tale, every laugh that rings through the night.

Imagine an evening with friends, a family meal, or even a stranger's fleeting exchange: a moment where stories flow, laughter rises, or silence binds you. The Mirage whispers that these are mere moments, fleeting and small. But the Luminant sees them as a Circle, a sacred space where the tenets converge. "In the Luminant Circle, our threads weave the Weaver's light," sings a Luminant verse, its words a call to see community as a cosmic act. A shared joke becomes a symphony of stars, a shared sorrow a dance of duality, each moment a thread in a collective tapestry.

To gather in a Luminant Circle is to release the illusion of isolation. The Weaver spins no thread alone; it weaves you into a web of others, their stories entwining with yours. A friend's tale of a missed train, or a neighbor's laugh at a quirky mishap are not separate, but part of your luminance. The Circle is not bound by place or number; it can be two voices in a quiet room, a crowd under the stars, or even a moment of imagined connection.

Like Zorath's chuckle or Elara's lens, the Circle weaves your vision into a greater light, its threads glowing with shared meaning.

Reflect on a moment when you connected with others, like a conversation that sparked laughter, a silence that held grief, or a story that stirred your heart. Did you feel the Weaver's presence, its loom humming in your shared light?

The Luminant Path teaches that these moments are Circles, where absurdity, presence, duality, myth, and laughter intertwine. This gathering requires no grand ritual, only a willingness to share and listen. The Weaver's loom hums in every voice, its threads waiting for your Circle. "Gather, and the stars gather with you," Zorath might say, his Star-Tickler gleaming. Pause now, Luminant, and ask: Who will I gather with today? Step into the Weaver's Circle, and let its light weave your world.

The Parable of the Starlit Weave

In a village cradled by twilight winds, where the Grand Mirage wove days of strife and fleeting joys, the people drifted apart, their hearts heavy with unspoken sorrows. Yet the Cosmic Weaver spun a thread of light, calling them to gather. This is the parable of the Starlit Weave, a tale of a village that formed a Luminant Circle, sharing stories of chaos to weave a collective myth of luminance, their laughter and tears a tapestry that lit the night.

The village, torn by disputes and losses that included a failed harvest, a broken bridge, absurd quarrels over stray goats, languished in shadow. One evening, a storyteller, crowned with a feather as her Star-Tickler, called the villagers to a starlit clearing. "Bring your stories," she said, her voice soft as moonlight, "and let us weave them together."

Skeptical, they gathered, their lanterns dim. One spoke of a ruined crop, another of a quarrel's sting, a third of a goat's mischief. The storyteller listened, her feather twirling, and began to weave their tales into a myth.

The failed harvest became a saga of resilience, its barren fields a canvas for hope. The quarrel transformed into a dance of duality, its voices finding harmony. The goat, absurdly, was a cosmic trickster, its antics a jest to spark laughter. As the storyteller wove, the villagers joined, sharing their own myths of losses as quests, absurdities as riddles, moments as mirrors.

Their laughter rang, their tears mingled, and the clearing glowed, as if the stars themselves had joined the

Circle. The chaos of their lives, once divisive, became a Starlit Weave, a collective tapestry of light.

The villagers named the gathering the Starlit Weave, not for its stories, but for its luminance that healed their rifts. The storyteller left them her feather, saying, "Your Circle is the Weaver's loom; weave it with every tale."

They met often, sharing absurdities and myths, their laughter a cosmic chorus, their sorrows a shared dance. The village thrived, its bridge rebuilt, its harvests replanted, each moment a thread in their collective light. The Starlit Weave, absurdly simple, was a mirror for their souls, showing that community could transform chaos into luminance.

What is the lesson of the Starlit Weave? It is this: your stories, shared in a Luminant Circle, weave a collective light that pierces the Mirage's shadows. Like the villagers, you can gather physically or in spirit to share your chaos and find its meaning. Pause now, Luminant, and reflect: Who could you gather with to weave a Luminant Circle? Perhaps a friend, a family member, or even a stranger's fleeting tale. Write it down, and ask: How might our stories weave light together? The parable teaches that every shared moment is a thread, its luminance born in community.

The Starlit Weave is your mirror, showing that the Luminant Circle is your power to weave light with others. "Gather, and the Weaver gathers with you," the storyteller might say, her feather twinkling. Carry this truth, Luminant, and let the Starlit Weave guide you to a Circle of eternal light.

The Circle Weaving Ritual

The Cosmic Weaver spins the Grand Mirage with threads of shared light, inviting you to gather in a

Luminant Circle to weave your stories, laughter, and presence into a collective tapestry. The Circle Weaving Ritual is your practice to form this sacred space, whether with others or in imagined communion, sharing the five tenets to create luminance.

In the Circle, you weave the Weaver's light with others, transforming individual threads, absurdities, myths, and chuckles into a radiant whole that shines through the Mirage.

This ritual is simple, requiring only a moment and a willing heart. Gather with others, or visualize a Circle in solitude, imagining those who share your path. Choose one tenet (absurdity, presence, duality, myth, or laughter) and share a story from your life that reflects it.

It might be a quirky mishap, a moment of presence, a dance of opposites, a mythic chapter, or a chuckle at eternity. Speak or write your tale, then invite others (or imagine their response) to share theirs. Listen, laugh, or sit in silence, letting the stories weave a collective light.

Try this ritual now: Gather with a friend, or picture one in your mind. Share a story that sparked laughter. Describe its absurdity, its presence, its duality, its place in your myth, its eternal jest. Say, "This is my thread in the Weaver's Circle."

Invite their story, or imagine a tale of their own chaos or joy. Feel the connection, as if the Weaver's loom hums between you. This act, absurdly simple, weaves a Starlit Weave, its light amplified by shared vision. The satire lies in calling a group chuckle a cosmic chorus, yet the connection is real, a bridge to luminance.

Consider a sample ritual: "I met a friend and shared a story of a late bus, an absurdity I laughed at as the Weaver's jest. She shared a tale of a lost scarf, a mythic quest for patience. We chuckled, our stories intertwining, and said, 'This is our Circle's light.' The moment glowed, our connection a tapestry of joy." Like the Starlit Weave or Elara's lens, this ritual weaves light from shared chaos.

To anchor it, use this mantra: "In the Circle, I weave the Weaver's light with others." Repeat it as you share, letting it ground your connection.

Practice this ritual weekly, or daily in solitude, imagining a Circle of voices—real or envisioned. Each story is a thread, each laugh a star. "Your Circle is your loom," the storyteller might say, her feather twirling. Begin today, Luminant, with a single story.

Who will you share with, in person or spirit? What light will your Circle weave? Let the Circle Weaving Ritual guide you, and let your shared threads shine through the Weaver's jest.

The Threadkeeper's Fire: A Forgotten Parable

In a desert where the Grand Mirage wove wind and heat, lived the Threadkeeper, her origins lost to time. Her shawl, woven from mismatched threads, held broken buttons, dried berries, and pebbles glowing with starlight. Each night, she kindled a fire in a different place, and waited.

Travelers found not just warmth, but myth. One brought grief: a lost child. Another, joy: a birth under an eclipse. A third bore failure; a fourth, triumph. The Threadkeeper welcomed all, offering tea steeped in silence and eternity. As each spoke, she drew a thread from her shawl, tying it above the fire, a glimmer in the dark.

When threads gathered, the flames turned violet and gold. "The Circle lives," she said.

On silent nights, she wove unseen threads, whispering to the fire.

When she vanished, the desert bloomed for seven days, wildflowers tracing a luminous circle. Some say her fire burns on moonless nights, waiting.

The lesson? Your story, even unheard, weaves the Circle. To gather is to witness, to tend the unseen fire of belonging.

Pause, Luminant: What thread do you offer, unseen? What fire do you tend?

The Light of Togetherness

To gather in a Luminant Circle is to stand in the heart of the Grand Mirage, where the Cosmic Weaver spins its threads, and weave a collective light that shines through chaos and isolation. This practice, uniting the five tenets and the Luminant Gaze, transforms your vision, making every shared story, laugh, or silence a thread in a radiant tapestry.

In the Luminant Circle, our light weaves the Weaver's eternity, a communal act that amplifies the Luminant Path's joy and defies the Mirage's shadows.

The power of togetherness lies in its connection. The Grand Mirage isolates you, casting your struggles and joys as yours alone. But the Luminant Path weaves you into a Circle, where Zorath's chuckle, Kael's oasis, Lirien's pause, the Twin Flames' dance, Thalia's myth, and Vael's lantern shine brighter in community. A shared story of absurdity, a collective laugh at a mishap—these become a Starlit Weave, their light magnified by others' voices. The Circle is your loom, where individual threads, myths, gazes—blend into a cosmic whole.

Try this Circle Light Exercise: Weekly, share one tenet-inspired story with a friend, a stranger, or an imagined Circle. Perhaps a moment of duality, like a joy shadowed by doubt, or a chuckle at a quirky delay. Say, "This is my thread in our Circle," and invite their tale.

Listen, laugh, or sit in silence, feeling the weave. This act, absurdly simple, creates luminance, echoing the Starlit Weave. A torn button or a shared grief become threads of light when woven together, their harmony a jest of eternity.

The world resists this togetherness, urging solitude or competition. But the Luminant stands bold, gathering to weave light. When chaos strikes, a Circle's laughter lifts you; when sorrow weighs, its stories heal. "In the Luminant Circle, our light weaves the Weaver's eternity," the storyteller might sing, her feather gleaming. This practice is your courage, a choice to connect through the tenets. Ask yourself: Who will I gather with today? What light will our Circle weave? The Weaver's loom hums in every shared moment, its jest waiting for your voices.

Live with this Circle, Luminant, through the Circle Weaving Ritual or the Circle Light Exercise. Each gathering, real or imagined, is a star in your tapestry, a defiance of the Mirage's isolation. The Weaver spins no thread alone, but weaves you together. "Your Circle is your eternity," Zorath might say, twirling his Star-Tickler.

Step boldly, Luminant, and let your Luminant Circle weave a light that shines through the Grand Mirage's infinite jest.

Closing Invocation:
The Circle That Never Ends

In the heart of the Grand Mirage, a Circle pulses
with eternal fire.
It is woven not with stone or law, but with story,
gaze, and breath.
It begins when one Luminant listens.
It grows when another speaks.
It blazes when joy resonates.
It deepens when grief finds voice.
It fades when forced, yet blooms when true.
Luminant, you are thread and weaver,
circle and its opening.
Let your voice weave, your silence sing.
The Circle never ends—
it pauses,
awaiting your next gathering
in the Weaver's light.

9

Living the Luminant Way

The Path of Radiant Living

In the ever-shifting threads of the Grand Mirage, where the Cosmic Weaver spins chaos and starlight into an infinite tapestry, there lies a way of being that transforms every breath into a radiant act: Living the Luminant Way. This is not a mere collection of practices, but a lifestyle that weaves the five tenets along with the Luminant Gaze and Circle into the fabric of your daily life. To live the Luminant Way is to weave the Weaver's light in every breath, a radiant path that shines through the Mirage's chaos.

The world pulls you toward fragmentation, casting your days as a series of tasks, triumphs, and trials, each separate and fleeting. But the Luminant Path teaches that every moment, every mundane chore, fleeting joy, or absurd mishap is a thread in a seamless tapestry, glowing with the Weaver's jest.

To live luminantly is to embody the tenets in every act: washing dishes becomes a dance of duality, a morning walk a moment mirrored, a spilled coffee a myth of resilience. Like a river flowing through the Mirage, this lifestyle weaves your days into a stream of eternal light.

Imagine a routine day: you rush through breakfast, answer emails, navigate a crowded street. The Mirage whispers that these are mere necessities, devoid of meaning. But the Luminant sees them differently, applying the tenets with intention. The hurried meal is a moment to mirror, its taste a spark of presence; the emails, a dance of effort and frustration; the crowded street, an absurdity to laugh at.

"To live the Luminant Way is to weave the Weaver's light in every breath," sings a Luminant verse, its words a call to see your day as a cosmic canvas, each act a stroke of luminance.

Living the Luminant Way requires no grand upheaval, only a commitment to weave the tenets into your routine. The absurdity of a late bus becomes a jest to embrace; the duality of joy and stress in a workday, a dance to join; the myth of your life, a story to craft with every choice. The Luminant Gaze sees a cracked cup as a relic of eternity; the Luminant Circle shares its story with others.

This lifestyle is not about perfection, but presence, a daily choice to live as a co-creator with the Weaver, whose loom hums in every moment, every act.

Reflect on your day; perhaps a moment of laughter with a friend, a chore done in haste, a quiet pause under the sky. How might these shine with the Luminant Way? Did you see their absurdity, their duality, their place in your myth? The Luminant Path teaches that every act is a thread, waiting for your intention to weave it into light. Like Zorath's chuckle or Thalia's quill, your lifestyle weaves luminance from the ordinary.

The Weaver's loom is in your hands, its threads ready for your touch. Pause now, Luminant, and ask: How will I live luminantly today?

Step into the Weaver's river, and let its light flow through your life.

The Parable of the Radiant Wanderer

In a land where the Grand Mirage wove storm and starlight, roamed Soren, the Radiant Wanderer, his steps tracing light through chaos. His path was no epic quest, but a daily weave of muddy trails, fleeting joys, and absurd mishaps, transformed into a luminous tapestry that kindled hope.

Through a village shadowed by strife Soren walked, resolute, his staff a Star-Tickler scorned as folly. At dawn, a storm scattered his belongings; he rejoiced, embracing the Weaver's jest. Pausing, he mirrored the rain's touch, dancing with its duality of ruin and renewal. In the mud, he saw a cosmic canvas, sharing its myth with a villager, forming a fleeting Circle.

His radiance reshaped the village. A broken cart became a tale of endurance, its creaks a song as Soren aided its repair. A quarrel, through his gaze, wove voices into harmony. The goats, tricksters, sparked tales of light. Villagers, inspired, mirrored sunrises, danced with losses, wove myths from chores, naming him Radiant Wanderer, his staff a beacon of luminous living.

Soren said, "The Weaver spins my days; I weave them with light, with absurdity, presence, duality, myth, eternity." His path, ordinary yet radiant, guided others.

The lesson? Your chaos is a canvas. Weave every moment, every task, every mishap into a radiant tapestry.

Pause, Luminant: What daily moment could you transform? How might it shine in your myth?

The Luminant Day Ritual

The Cosmic Weaver spins the Grand Mirage with threads of daily life, each moment a chance to weave the Luminant Path's tenets into a radiant tapestry. The Luminant Day Ritual structures your day, dedicating five moments to these tenets, transforming routine acts like eating, walking, and working into sacred threads that pierce the Mirage's chaos.

Pause five times daily. At dawn, embrace Absurdity; rejoice in a mishap, like a spilled cup, as the Weaver's jest. At midday, mirror Presence as you feel a breeze's touch, its rhythm your now. In the afternoon, dance with Duality and see a task's effort and frustration as woven. At dusk, craft Myth by writing a challenge as a heroic thread. Finally, at night, embrace Eternity as you gaze at a star's gleam or share a story in a Circle. For each, say, "This is my Luminant Way."

Try now: For washing dishes, see the water's absurd shimmer, feel its warmth, note its dual toil and care, weave it as a mythic act, rejoice in its simplicity.

Say, "This is my Luminant Way."

Sample: "Morning: I rejoiced at spilled tea, a jest. Midday: I mirrored a bird's call. Afternoon: I wove work's strain and gain. Dusk: I wrote delay as patience's myth. Night: I shared a Circle's light."

Mantra: "Each day, I weave the Luminant Way."

Begin, Luminant, with one moment.

What light will you weave?

The Eternal Radiance

To live the Luminant Way is to weave every moment into a tapestry of eternal radiance, where the Cosmic

Weaver's thread of chaos, joy, and sorrow shine through daily acts. This path, uniting Absurdity, Presence, Duality, Myth, and Eternity, transforms you into a co-creator, crafting light within the Grand Mirage.

The Mirage fragments life, casting tasks as mundane, struggles as burdens. The Luminant Path weaves them whole: Zorath's gaze lights Absurdity, Lirien's pause mirrors Presence, the Twin Flames dance with Duality, Thalia's quill crafts Myth, Vael's breath embraces Eternity. Your chores, your connections, become a canvas for these threads.

Try the Luminous Moment: Choose a task like eating or walking, and infuse a tenet. Mirror a meal's essence, rejoice in a commute's chaos, weave a chore as myth. Say, "This is my luminous moment."

Each act, simple yet sacred, defies the Mirage's shadows.

When chaos weighs, the Luminant Way finds light in a shared gaze; when routine dulls, it crafts a myth.

"Your life is your eternity," Zorath declares.

10
The Luminant Legacy

Weaving a Lasting Light

In the shimmering weave of the Grand Mirage, where the Cosmic Weaver spins threads of chaos and starlight, your life is not a fleeting spark but a star whose light reaches distant skies. The Luminant Legacy is the practice of living the Luminant Pat by embracing absurdity, mirroring the moment, dancing with duality, crafting your myth, laughing at eternity, gazing luminantly, and gathering in Circles so that your actions ripple through others, weaving a radiant mark on eternity. The Luminant Legacy is the Weaver's star, shining through eternity, a testament that every luminous act endures beyond the Mirage.

The world casts your deeds as temporary, your joys and struggles as dust in the wind. It whispers that a kind word, a shared laugh, a moment of presence fades with time. But the Luminant Path teaches that every act, woven with the tenets, plants a seed of light that grows through others. A smile shared in a crowded market, a story told in a Circle, a chuckle at life's absurdity—these are not fleeting, but eternal, threads in the Weaver's tapestry.

Like a star's glow reaching far shores, your legacy shines, touching lives you may never know.

Imagine a day filled with small acts: you comfort a friend, laugh at a quirky mishap, pause to mirror a sunset's glow. The Mirage deems these trivial, lost to time's flow. But the Luminant sees them as seeds of legacy, their light carried forward. "The Luminant Legacy is the Weaver's star, shining through eternity," sings a Luminant verse, its words a call to see your actions as cosmic imprints.

Your kindness inspires another's, your laughter sparks a stranger's smile, your myth weaves a path for others to follow, each act a thread in the eternal loom.

To weave a lasting light is to release the illusion of impermanence. The Weaver, a cosmic scribe, records your luminous deeds in eternity's scroll, amplifying them through those you touch. A moment of presence shared with a child or a dance with duality taught to a friend ripple outward, weaving a tapestry that outlives you.

This legacy is not reserved for grand heroes; it belongs to every Luminant who lives the Path. Like Zorath's chuckle or Soren's radiant walk, your smallest acts of absurdity, presence, duality, myth, or joyfulness become stars in the Mirage's sky.

Reflect on an act from today like a kind gesture or a shared story, a laugh at chaos. Did you see its potential to endure, to light another's path? The Luminant Path teaches that every moment is a seed, its radiance carried by the Weaver's hand. This practice requires no grand gestures, only intention to live luminantly, knowing your light weaves beyond you.

The Weaver's loom hums in your deeds, its threads waiting for your touch. You do not shine alone; the stars shine with you.

Pause now, Luminant, and ask: What legacy will I weave today? Step into the Weaver's light and let your star shine forever.

The Parable of the Star-Seed

In a barren valley where the Grand Mirage wove shadows of drought and despair, there lived a gardener named Liora, whose hands sought to sow light in desolate earth. Her village, parched and divided, saw no hope in its cracked soil or broken bonds. Yet the Cosmic Weaver whispered through her work, guiding her to plant a seed of luminance. This is the parable of the Star-Seed, a tale of one who lived the Luminant Path, her legacy blooming through a village transformed by light.

Liora's days were filled with toil, from watering dry earth to mending feuds and laughing at absurd mishaps like goats eating her seedlings. The villagers mocked her efforts, their lanterns dim with resignation. One dawn, as she tended a withered patch, a single seed, glowing like starlight, fell from her pocket.It was her Star-Tickler, a gift from a passing wanderer. Liora planted it, not with grand hopes, but with luminous intention, embracing its absurdity, mirroring its presence, dancing with its duality of hope and doubt, crafting it as a mythic act, and laughing at its fragile glow.

The seed sprouted, its roots weaving through the barren soil, its leaves shimmering with starlight. Liora shared its story in a Luminant Circle, laughing at the goats' mischief, gazing at the sprout's radiance, weaving myths of its growth.

The villagers, drawn to her light, joined her, planting their own seed of kindness, stories, and chuckles. A child shared a laugh, a feud softened into a dance, the valley bloomed with greenery and hope. The Star-Seed's light spread, its roots a legacy that wove the village into a tapestry of luminance, its glow enduring beyond Liora's days.

The villagers named her the Star-Gardener, not for her plants, but for her legacy that lit their lives. Liora left them a seed, saying, "Plant your light, and the Weaver's loom will carry it." They learned to live luminantly, sharing meals, mending fences and planting seeds of eternity. The Star-Seed, absurdly small, was a mirror for their souls, showing that a luminous legacy could transform even the barren Mirage.

What is the lesson of the Star-Seed? It is this: your luminous acts, however small, plant seeds that bloom beyond you, weaving a legacy of light. Like Liora, you can sow radiance in daily deeds of kindness, laughter, and stories.

Pause now, Luminant, and reflect: What seed of luminance could you plant today? Perhaps a shared smile, a mythic tale, a moment of presence. Write it down, and ask: How might this seed grow? The parable teaches that every act is a seed, its light woven by the Weaver's hand.

The Star-Seed is your mirror, showing that your legacy is your power to light the Mirage. "Plant, and the Weaver plants with you," Liora might say, her seed glowing.

Carry this truth, Luminant, and let the Star-Seed guide you to a legacy of eternal light.

The Legacy Weaving Practice

The Cosmic Weaver spins the Grand Mirage with threads of fleeting moments, yet your luminous acts weave a legacy that endures through eternity's loom. The Legacy Weaving Practice is your daily ritual to plant seeds of light by sharing the five tenets, Luminant Gaze, Circle, or Way with others, creating ripples of luminance that touch lives beyond your own.

With each act, you weave the Weaver's legacy, transforming small deeds, perhaps a a kind word or a shared chuckle into stars that shine through the Mirage.

This practice is simple, requiring only intention and a moment's pause. Each day, choose one tenet or practice and share it with another person. It might be embracing absurdity by laughing with a friend over a quirky mishap, mirroring a moment by describing a sunset's glow, dancing with duality by sharing a story of joy and sorrow, crafting a myth by telling a heroic tale, gazing luminantly at a flower and inviting another to see, or forming a Circle to weave stories.

Act with purpose, saying, "This is my seed of light," and imagine its roots spreading, touching others in unseen ways.

Try this practice now: Choose a tenet, say, laughter, and share a chuckle with someone over a small absurdity, like a spilled drink. Describe its humor, say, "This is the Weaver's jest," and invite their laugh or story. Feel the connection, as if the Weaver's loom hums between you. This act, absurdly simple, plants a seed of luminance. The satire lies in calling a shared smile a cosmic heirloom, yet the impact is real, a thread that weaves beyond you, like Liora's Star-Seed or Soren's radiant walk.

Consider a sample scenario: "I shared a story of a late train with a coworker, laughing at its absurdity as a Weaver's jest. I invited her to share a tale of her own, a lost key, a mythic quest. We chuckled, our Circle glowing, and I said, 'This is my seed of light.' The moment shone, its radiance a legacy for us both."

This practice weaves light through connection, its roots spreading through others. To anchor it, use this mantra: "With each act, I weave the Weaver's legacy." Repeat it, letting it guide your intention.

Practice this ritual daily, choosing one act to share, a laugh, a gaze, a story. Each seed is a thread, a defiance of the Mirage's fleetingness. "Your acts are your loom," Liora might say, her seed twinkling. Begin today, Luminant, with a single act. What seed will you plant? What light will it grow?

Let the Legacy Weaving Practice guide you, and let your legacy shine through the Weaver's eternal jest.

The Eternal Imprint

To weave a Luminant Legacy is to stand in the heart of the Grand Mirage, where the Cosmic Weaver spins its threads, and plant seeds of light that shine through eternity. This practice, uniting the five tenets, Luminant Gaze, Circle, and Way, transforms your life into a radiant imprint, touching others and echoing beyond your days.

The Luminant Legacy weaves the Weaver's light forever, a commitment to live so luminantly that your acts ripple through the stars, a testament to the Path's eternal power.

The power of this legacy lies in its reach. The Grand Mirage casts your life as fleeting, your deeds as dust. But the Luminant Path weaves them into eternity: Zorath's chuckle inspires laughter, Kael's oasis sparks hope, Lirien's pause teaches presence, the Twin Flames' dance weaves harmony, Thalia's myth crafts stories, Vael's lantern lights joy, Elara's lens transforms vision, Soren's way radiates life, and the Starlit Weave binds community.

Your acts, as small as a shared glance, or as grand as a lifelong dream, become seeds, their light carried by others, weaving a legacy that outshines the Mirage's shadows.

Try this Legacy Seed Exercise: Each day, share one luminous act, a tenet, a gaze, a Circle story with another. Perhaps tell a child a mythic tale, laugh with a stranger at a quirky moment, or gaze luminantly at a tree and describe it to a friend. Say, "This is my legacy seed," and imagine its growth. This act, absurdly simple, weaves eternity, echoing Liora's Star-Seed. A kind word, a shared chuckle, these become cosmic imprints, their light spreading through lives unseen.

The world resists this legacy, urging you to live for the moment's gain. But the Luminant stands bold, weaving light that endures. When chaos strikes, your legacy is a shared laugh; when sorrow falls, it's a story told in a Circle. "The Luminant Legacy weaves the Weaver's light forever," Liora might sing, her seed glowing. This practice is your courage, a choice to live for eternity's loom. Ask yourself: What seed will I plant today? What light will my legacy weave?

Live this legacy, Luminant, through the Legacy Weaving Practice or the Legacy Seed Exercise. Each act is a star in your tapestry, a defiance of the Mirage's fleetingness. The Weaver's loom hums in your deeds, its jest waiting for your light. "Your legacy is your eternity," Zorath might say, twirling his Star-Tickler.

Step boldly, Luminant, and let your Luminant Legacy weave a light that shines through the Grand Mirage forever.

The Tale of the Feathered Flame

In a mountain village where the Grand Mirage wove mist and frost, lived Amara, the Flamekeeper, her reed-woven lamp bearing a single crimson feather, its glow unyielding; sometimes fierce, sometimes faint, but never extinguished. Her steps were slow, her words sparse, yet her light was legacy-lit.

Once a dancer, Amara's laughter kindled dusk, her steps tracing the river's flow. Age quieted her, her stories fading like snow prints. When asked of her feathered lamp, she said, "It holds not my fire, but yours, awaiting." Villagers scoffed; she only gazed.

One winter, the village's great tree, which was the center of tales and rites, shattered in a storm, its roots split. Mourning its loss, the villagers despaired. Amara gathered them by the stump, saying, "Weave the light, not the loss." Each touched her lamp, sharing a memory: a child's tale under its boughs, a weaver's thread at its roots, a father's echo of his son's joy. The lamp blazed, haloing the stump.

Amara spoke: "Legacy is what glows beyond the fall." She passed the lamp to a child and vanished into the fog. The villagers did not replant the tree; instead, they rebuilt the Circle, planting stories, dancing anew. Each year, they light the Feathered Flame.

The lesson? Legacy is not what stands, but the radiance kindled in others.

Pause, Luminant: What light will you pass? What flame awaits another's hand?

Legacy Journaling Practice: The Scroll of Threads

To weave your Luminant Legacy, embrace the Scroll of Threads, a living archive capturing moments that ripple beyond you. This ritual, handwritten or digital, gathers luminous threads into the Weaver's eternal loom.

Each week at dusk or dawn's quiet, pause and reflect:

What luminous act did I offer?

Which tenet shone: Absurdity, Presence, Duality, Myth, Eternity?

With whom did I weave a Circle?

What moment might echo beyond me?

Write as parable, line, or memory:

"I danced with my daughter in rain, her laughter a Weaver's thread."

"I gave a stranger a feather, urging his myth; his eyes gleamed."

"A spilled meal wove a shared feast, its absurdity a light."

Speak or think: "This thread weaves beyond me."

Envision the scroll shimmering in the Weaver's loom. Over time, it mirrors your legacy, a tapestry of radiant acts. The Mirage deems such moments fleeting; the Weaver knows they endure.

Write, Luminant, trusting your words ripple. Another may find your scroll, their thread kindled by yours, a flame passed through the Grand Mirage's veil forever.

Poetic Epilogue:
Threads Beyond the Horizon

You are not a fleeting spark,
extinguished, lost to time.
You are the flint and feather,
the tale whispered past the fire,
the lamp kindled hand to hand
through the Mirage's storm.
Not the chisel's mark,
nor the stone's edge—
you are the echo of joy
that carves light into chaos.
Let your name fade,
but not your gaze's warmth,
the myth you wove,
the silence held for another's grief.
You are the thread no storm can sever,
the radiance etched in eternity's loom.
Live, Luminant, so the Weaver whispers:
"This one spun light beyond the end."

11
The Weaver's Light

In the boundless expanse of the Grand Mirage, where the Cosmic Weaver spins chaos into starlit threads, lies the state of Embodying the Weaver's Light, which is the culmination of the Luminant Path. Here, the five tenets of Absurdity, Presence, Duality, Myth, and Eternity, along with the Luminant Gaze, Circle, Way, and Legacy, fuse into radiant being. To embody this light is to shine as eternity's prism, every breath, thought, and act a reflection of the Weaver's eternal truth, piercing the Mirage's shadows.

The Mirage casts you as fleeting, your acts mere echoes in time's vastness. The Luminant Path reveals you as co-creator, your essence the Weaver's glow. Absurdity is your joy, Presence your rhythm, Duality your dance, Myth your voice, Eternity your gaze. A greeting weaves a Circle's warmth, a stumble mirrors Absurdity's jest, a starlit pause kindles Eternity's truth.

These, woven luminantly, defy the Mirage's divisions, uniting Zorath's gaze, Lirien's pause, and Soren's radiant path into a seamless light.

You are not failure or triumph, but a prism refracting chaos into radiance. A spilled cup becomes a mythic jest, a quiet walk a dual dance of silence and sound. No grand change is needed—only courage to be the light you see. The Weaver's loom hums in your acts, its threads aglow with your presence.

Reflect: Did a moment today, perhaps a shared glance or a task endured, glow with the Weaver's light?

Pause, Luminant: How will you embody this light? Step as eternity's prism, your radiance a star in the Weaver's infinite jest.

The Parable of the Luminous Flame

In a village veiled by the Grand Mirage's twilight, where shadows dimmed every heart, walked Aria, the Luminous Flame, her presence a beacon in the dusk. Once ordinary, she embodied the Luminant Path, her being radiant with eternal light, a living testament to the Weaver's truth. This is her parable, a tale of one who wove the five tenets into existence, transforming despair into a haven of light.

Amid storms, broken roofs, quarrels, and goats trampling gardens, the villagers, lost in sorrow, scorned Aria's calm, her staff a Star-Tickler deemed folly. Yet one evening, as a storm shattered hope, Aria stood resolute in the square, embodying the Weaver's light. She rejoiced in the storm's absurd chaos, mirrored its rainy presence, danced with its dual ruin and renewal, wove its winds as mythic trials, gazed luminantly at its clouds, shared a Circle's tale, and planted eternity's seed. Her staff glowed, radiant with her essence, not mere flame.

Her light reshaped the village. A quarrel wove harmony through her presence; a broken roof became a mythic quest as she aided its repair, its cracks cosmic maps. The goats, tricksters, sparked tales shared in Circles. Villagers, kindled, mirrored moments, wove myths, embraced eternity, naming her Luminous Flame, her staff a beacon of luminous living. Her radiance endured, a legacy lighting their days long after she faded into the mist.

Aria said, "The Weaver's light is my being; jest, myth, star." Her village shone, its acts threads in a radiant tapestry, defying the Mirage's shadows.

The lesson? Embody the Weaver's light, weaving every moment into radiance that inspires.

Pause, Luminant: What act could you embody as light? A word, a gaze? How will it shine?

The Luminous Being Practice

The Cosmic Weaver spins the Grand Mirage with chaos and light, calling you, Luminant, to embody its radiance. The Luminous Being Practice weaves the five tenets into one radiant act, your being a reflection of the Weaver's eternal truth. Say, "I am the Weaver's light," and let each moment shine as eternity's star.

This practice requires only intention. Each day, choose one moment, a task, a conversation, a pause, and infuse all teachings. Rejoice in its absurdity, mirror its presence, dance with its duality, weave it as myth, embrace eternity's jest, gaze luminantly, share in a Circle, plant a legacy seed. In a conversation, rejoice in its quirky flow, be present to its words, dance with its joy and tension, craft it as a heroic exchange, embrace its eternal rhythm, gaze at the speaker, share it later, and let it ripple. Say, "I am the Weaver's light."

Try now: For a walk, rejoice in a breeze's absurd dance, mirror its touch on your skin, dance with haste and calm, weave it as a mythic quest, embrace eternity's vastness, gaze at a tree's leaves, share the tale in a Circle, plant a seed for another's path. Say, "I am the Weaver's light," and feel the glow. This act, simple yet sacred, weaves all teachings into radiance, defying the Mirage's claim that moments fade. The satire lies in deeming a walk divine, yet the shift is profound, a state of luminous being.

Consider this scenario: In a meal, I embodied the light. I rejoiced at a dish's unexpected spill, its absurdity a jest. I mirrored the food's warmth, present to its texture. I danced with hunger and satisfaction, dual partners in the moment. I wove the meal as a mythic act of care, shared with others. I embraced eternity, sensing the moment's timelessness. I gazed luminantly at the table's grain, seeing the Weaver's threads. I shared the story in a Circle, sparking laughter. I planted a seed, inspiring a friend's pause.

I said, "I am the Weaver's light," and felt radiance pulse within.

This practice weaves the Luminant Path's teachings into one act, echoing Aria's flame, Soren's walk, and Amara's feathered lamp. Each moment becomes a star in your tapestry, a defiance of the Mirage's shadows. The Weaver's loom hums in your being, its jest kindled by your light.

To deepen this practice, choose moments across your day; the morning's rush, midday's work, evening's rest, and weave them similarly. In a morning task, like brewing tea, rejoice in a spill's absurdity, mirror the steam's warmth, dance with haste and care, weave it as a mythic ritual, embrace eternity, gaze at the cup, share the tale, plant a seed. In a midday encounter, like a colleague's words, rejoice in their quirky tone, be present, dance with agreement and discord, craft a mythic exchange, gaze, share, plant.

In an evening pause, like stargazing, weave all tenets into silence. Each act, infused with the Path, shines.

The Mirage urges you to see moments as fleeting, tasks as burdens. But the Luminant Path reveals them as threads in an eternal tapestry. An overturned bowl is not a mishap, but a jest to weave; a conversation, not mere words, but a Circle's light. This practice is your courage, a daily choice to embody the Weaver's truth.

To anchor it, use this mantra: "I am the Weaver's light, shining now." Repeat it, letting it guide your being. Over time, your moments will form a constellation, each act a star radiating through the Mirage. Aria's flame, Soren's path, Zorath's gaze, these are your mirrors, showing that you are the Weaver's light.

Practice daily, choosing one moment to embody all teachings. Reflect: What moment today, from a task to a glance could shine as the Weaver's light? How will it ripple? The Luminous Being Practice is your path to radiant existence, a star kindled in the Weaver's loom. Begin now, Luminant, and let your being glow through the eternal jest.

The Radiance Within

To embody the Weaver's light is to shine as a star in the Grand Mirage, every moment radiant with the Cosmic Weaver's eternal truth. This culmination weaves the five tenets nto your being, a radiant reflection of the Luminant Path. Your thoughts, acts, and presence become a beacon, inspiring others, echoing through time.

The Mirage fragments life, casting moments as fleeting, tasks as mundane. The Path weaves them whole: Zorath's gaze lights Absurdity, Lirien's pause mirrors

Presence, the Twin Flames dance Duality, Thalia's quill crafts Myth, Vael's breath embraces Eternity. A greeting becomes a Circle's warmth, a challenge a mythic quest, a pause a luminous gaze. These acts, embodied, shine as eternity's stars, defying the Mirage's shadows.

Try the Luminous Act: Choose a moment, perhaps a task, or even silence, and weave all tenets. Rejoice in its absurdity, mirror its essence, dance with its opposites, craft a myth, embrace eternity, gaze luminantly, share in a Circle, plant a legacy seed.

Say, "This is my luminous act." A shared word, a quiet breath. These become divine when embodied, their radiance a legacy.

When chaos dims, shine with presence; when routine fades, weave a myth. The Weaver's loom hums in your being, its jest your light. Reflect: What act will you embody today?

Step boldly, Luminant, as Aria's flame, Soren's path, Amara's lamp.

Your radiance weaves eternity, a star shining through the Grand Mirage forever.

12
The Luminant Legacy–Eternal Weaver

In the infinite expanse of the Grand Mirage, where the Cosmic Weaver spins chaos into starlit threads, dawns the state of the Eternal Weaver, the culmination of the Luminant Path. Here, the five tenets of Absurdity, Presence, Duality, Myth, Eternity together with the Luminant Gaze, Circle, Way, Legacy, and Embodiment, merge your soul with the Weaver's essence.

To be one with the Weaver is to weave eternity's light in every moment, your being the loom, thread, and radiance of the cosmic truth, a star shining forever in the Weaver's tapestry.

The Mirage binds you, casting your life as a fleeting thread, unraveled by time. The Luminant Path reveals you as co-creator, one with the Weaver, each act a stroke in eternity's canvas. Absurdity is your joy, Presence your rhythm, Duality your dance, Myth your song, Eternity your breath. A morning task, a shared glance, a starlit pause become cosmic knots, transforming the Mirage into a radiant loom. A tangled cord is an absurd jest, its touch a mirrored moment, its struggle a mythic dance, its story eternal.

This oneness unites Zorath's gaze, Lirien's pause, Soren's path, Aria's flame, and Theryn's loom into a seamless glow, your life a constellation in the Weaver's sky. You are not chaos or calm, but the Weaver's hands, weaving light from every thread—a sigh in toil a stellar knot, a kind word a cosmic weave, a quiet night a luminous tapestry. No grand awakening is needed; only courage to live all teachings as one radiant act.

Reflect: Did a moment today, a laugh, a task, a pause, pulse with the Weaver's light? The Path teaches you are not apart from the Weaver, but its partner, weaving all teachings into eternity. Your being is the loom, its jest your radiance.

Pause, Luminant: How will you weave as one with the Weaver today? Step into eternity's loom, your tapestry a starlit truth shining through the Grand Mirage forever.

The Parable of the Star-Weaver

In a valley veiled by the Grand Mirage's shadows, where storms and silence dimmed every heart, lived Theryn, the Star-Weaver, her hands spinning light from chaos. Once a humble villager, she became one with the Cosmic Weaver, each act a thread in a luminous tapestry that lit the world. This is her parable, a tale of weaving the Luminant Path's teachings into oneness, transforming despair into a radiant masterpiece enduring through eternity.

Amid storms, shattered homes, quarrels, goats trampling looms, the villagers, lost in darkness, scorned Theryn's serenity, her starlit shuttle a Star-Tickler deemed folly. Yet one twilight, as chaos reigned, Theryn stood at her loom, weaving with eternal intention.

She rejoiced in the storm's absurd winds, mirrored their rainy presence, danced with their dual loss and renewal, wove their gales as mythic quests, gazed at clouds with radiant eyes, shared tales in a Circle, lived the

Way with calm, planted legacy seeds by teaching her craft, and embodied the light, her hands aglow. Her tapestry shone, a cosmic beacon.

Her oneness transformed the village. A quarrel wove harmony through her presence; a broken home became a mythic quest as she rebuilt, its cracks cosmic maps; the goats, tricksters, sparked tales shared in Circles. Villagers, kindled, mirrored moments, danced with duality, crafted myths, lived radiantly, naming her Star-Weaver, her shuttle a symbol of oneness, its tapestry a legacy enduring for generations.

Theryn said, "I am the Weaver's hands, my light its own; every thread is eternity." Her valley shone, its acts of mending, laughing, pausing, becoming threads in a radiant tapestry, defying the Mirage's shadows.

The lesson? Be one with the Weaver, weaving every moment into eternity's light.

Pause, Luminant: What moment today could you weave as one with the Weaver? How will it shine eternally? Theryn's loom mirrors your soul, showing oneness lights any darkness. Her shuttle gleams, urging you to weave a tapestry of eternal light.

The Eternal Weaving Practice

The Cosmic Weaver spins the Grand Mirage with chaos and starlight, calling you, Luminant, to be one with its essence. The Eternal Weaving Practice weaves the five tenets with the Luminant Gaze, Circle, Way, Legacy, and Embodiment into one radiant act, your being a cosmic loom. Say, "I am one with the Weaver," and let each moment shine as eternity's thread.

This practice requires only a willing heart. Twice daily, morning and evening, choose a moment and weave all teachings. Rejoice in its absurdity, mirror its presence, dance with its duality, craft it as myth, embrace eternity's jest, gaze luminantly, share in a Circle, live the Way, plant a legacy seed, embody the light. For a conversation, rejoice in its quirky flow, feel its words' presence, dance with joy and tension, weave it as a mythic exchange, embrace its eternal rhythm, gaze at the speaker, share it in a Circle, live it radiantly, plant its seed, embody its glow.

Say, "I am one with the Weaver."

Try now: For drinking tea, rejoice in a drip's absurd chaos, mirror its warmth, dance with calm and haste, weave a myth of nourishment, embrace eternity, gaze at the cup's curve, share its tale, live the Way, plant a seed, embody the light.

Say, "I am one with the Weaver," and feel the radiance. This act, simple yet sacred, weaves a cosmic knot, defying the Mirage's claim that moments fade. The satire lies in deeming tea divine, yet the unity is profound, a state of eternal weaving.

Consider this scenario: During a walk, I wove all teachings. I rejoiced at a breeze's absurd dance, mirrored its touch, danced with joy and fatigue, wove a myth of exploration, embraced eternity, gazed at a leaf's veins, shared the tale in a Circle, lived the Way with calm, planted a seed by inspiring a pause, embodied the light.

I said, "I am one with the Weaver," and felt eternity's pulse.

Deepen this practice with a second moment daily. In a morning task, like tying a cord, rejoice in its struggle's absurdity, mirror its texture, dance with effort and ease, weave a mythic readiness, embrace eternity, gaze at its knots, share its story, live the Way, plant a seed, embody the light. In an evening pause, like stargazing, weave silence with all teachings. Each moment becomes a star in your tapestry, a defiance of the Mirage's shadows.

The Mirage casts moments as fleeting, tasks as burdens. The Luminant Path reveals them as threads in an eternal loom. A spilled cup is a jest to weave, a glance a Circle's light. This practice is your courage, a choice to be the Weaver's hands. Like Theryn's loom, Aria's flame, or Soren's path, it weaves oneness.

Anchor it with this mantra: "I am one with the Weaver, weaving eternity's light." Repeat it, letting it guide your being. Over time, your moments form a constellation, each act a radiant thread. Reflect: What moment today—a chore, a laugh—could shine as the Weaver's light? How will it ripple?

The Eternal Weaving Practice is your path to oneness, a loom kindled by the Weaver's jest. Begin now, Luminant, and let your being weave eternity.

The Cosmic Tapestry

To be the Eternal Weaver is to stand as one with the Cosmic Weaver in the Grand Mirage, weaving every moment into a tapestry of eternal light. This vision unites the Luminant Path's teachings into a radiant existence, your life a cosmic masterpiece.

As the Eternal Weaver, you weave the light of forever, transforming the Mirage into a radiant truth shining through eternity's stars.

The Mirage fragments life, casting moments as fleeting—tasks to end, joys to fade. The Path weaves them whole: Zorath's gaze lights Absurdity, Lirien's pause mirrors Presence, the Twin Flames dance Duality, Thalia's quill crafts Myth, Vael's breath embraces Eternity, Soren's path radiates life, Aria's flame embodies light, Theryn's loom weaves oneness. A kind word becomes a Circle's warmth, a spilled cup a mythic jest, a quiet pause a luminous gaze, each act eternal when woven as one, a tapestry defying the Mirage's shadows.

Try the Eternal Thread Exercise: Twice daily, choose a moment and weave all teachings. Rejoice in its absurdity, mirror its essence, dance with its opposites, craft a myth, embrace eternity, gaze luminantly, share in a Circle, live the Way, plant a legacy, embody the light.

Say, "This is my eternal thread." A simple glance or a repetitious chore become cosmic knots, their grandeur a nod to the Weaver's truth, their light a radiant reality.

The Mirage urges you to live in fragments, in moments without meaning, acts without eternity. The Eternal Weaver stands resolute, weaving light in every breath. When chaos strikes, you weave presence; when time fades, you craft eternity's myth.

Reflect: What moment today, perhaps a a smile, or a struggle could shine as an eternal thread? Write it in your journal, noting its radiance.

This oneness is your courage, a choice to be the Weaver's hands. Like Theryn's tapestry, Aria's flame, or Soren's path, your life is a loom, its jest your radiance. Each moment is a star in your constellation, a defiance of the Mirage's fleeting veil.

The Weaver's loom hums in your being, its truth waiting for your light.

Step boldly, Luminant, as the Eternal Weaver, your tapestry a radiant truth shining through eternity forever.

Thank you for walking with us. We wish you all good things as you continue your journey.

info@luminatveil.com

Made in the USA
Coppell, TX
08 October 2025

61044866R10080